TAKE
THE
STAND

TAKE
THE
STAND

CHARLES B. GRAHAM

Foreword by James Reimann

BROADMAN
&HOLMAN
PUBLISHERS

Nashville, Tennessee

Published by:
Broadman & Holman Publishers, Nashville, Tennessee

Acquisitions & Development Editor:
Vicki Crumpton

Interior Design:
Steven Boyd

Printed in the United States of America

4262-67
0-8054-6267-8

Dewey Decimal Classification: 248.84
Subject Heading: CHRISTIAN LIFE
Library of Congress Card Catalog Number: 96-19677

Unless otherwise noted, Scripture quotations are from the Holy Bible, New International Version, copyright © 1973, 1978, 1984 by International Bible Society.

Library of Congress Cataloging-in-Publication Data
Graham, Charles B.
   Take the stand! / Charles B. Graham
   p.   cm.
   ISBN 0-8054-6267-8 (pb)
   1. Witness bearing (Christianity).   2.Christian life—Baptist authors.
   3. Graham, Charles B., 1954–
   I. Title.
   BV4520.G66   1996
   248.4'86—dc20

   96-19677
   CIP

96 97 98 99 00 5 4 3 2 1

First and foremost, this book is dedicated to my Lord and Savior, Jesus Christ. The following pages developed from my prayer journal, a collection of conversations I have had with God. It is my prayer that the message of this book will serve only to glorify Him and bring honor to His name.

Second, to the men, women, and ministries of Focus on the Family, Promise Keepers, Precept Ministries, Solid Rock Ministries, Christian Legal Society, and especially the Christian Life Commission of the Southern Baptist Convention, who teach, remind, encourage, caution, challenge, and lead us to withstand the ridicule, hatred, hypocrisy, and allure of *this* world so that we may be the people God wants in *His*.

And lastly, to the reader: pray for wisdom, search for understanding, apply the truth that God reveals, and live your life in a manner worthy of the One who gave up His for you. Do not be ashamed. *Take the stand.*

c∞ɔ

Contents

Foreword

Whatever happened to a faith that permeates every facet of society? Where are the Christians today whose faith makes a difference everyday and everywhere they go? How did we ever get to the point in this country where Christians seem to simply blend into their surroundings? Why is it that there is statistically little difference between believers and nonbelievers when looking at the social ills we suffer in society?

The answer is that Christians, especially over the last few years, have taken a much more casual approach to Christianity. We make excuses for ourselves, such as, "Well, I wouldn't want to come on too strong," or, "I believe my life should be my witness." Therefore, we continually forego opportunities outside the church to share the gospel and allow our convictions and ethics to be compromised in the workplace for fear of "offending" someone.

As I am writing these words, I am thinking back over the past ten years, since I first met Chuck Graham. Shortly after we met, he began representing me as my business and personal attorney. I sensed immediately that here was someone who not only *knew* the Lord, but also *lived* his faith. Some would say, "An amazing thing for a lawyer!" Since then we have grown to be close friends, sharing many times of work, prayer, victories, defeats, golf (speaking of defeats), and even a few good-natured practical jokes.

Today, as a writer and editor myself, I know the years of work that go into the preparation of a worthwhile book. Thousands of Christian books are published every year and many have no impact on those who read them. I trust this will not be one of those books, but that is actually up to you as the reader.

Take the Stand is a call to the church to be the church—every day! It is a call for us who bear the name of Christ to be salt and light—everywhere! It is a practical guide, based on the truth of God's Word that, *if applied,* will make a difference in your life, your home, your church, your business, your community, and your world. It is a call to forsake the casual Christianity that has become so prevalent today.

Is it your desire to reclaim the zeal you had when you first believed? Are you frustrated with your business-as-usual Christianity? If so, ahead is a straightforward approach to return to the basics of the faith that are so neglected or forgotten today. The apostle Paul said, "My determined purpose is that I may know Him" (Phil. 3:10, AMP). If your desire is to know Christ better and to be a more powerful witness for Him, then read on.

Remember, however, that *applying* the truth in this book is what will make the difference in your life and in the world around you. It is up to you to *take the stand.*

James Reimann
Editor, *My Utmost for His Highest,* Updated Edition
October 1996

Acknowledgments

It is with a grateful heart that I thank the following people. Your love, support, prayers, insight, and encouragement were much needed and appreciated.

My wonderful wife, Beverly, and our children, Chase, Mallory, and Matthew, for putting up with me during the years of work, frustration, fear, and joy. I love you very much.

Ronald G. Hanie, pastor, White Oak Hills Baptist Church, for solid teaching, courageous preaching, and showing me a love for Christ greater than I had ever known.

Jim and Pam Reimann, for being dear friends and great encouragers.

Frank Stanley, Steve Smith, Bob Bruce, Ralph Sackett, Charles Phillips, Linda Smith, and Robert Crout, for your kindness in reviewing drafts and giving me valuable input and guidance.

The board of directors of Solid Rock Ministries, Conyers, Georgia (Butch Rumble, Tony Breedlove, Martin Chandler, Ben Gatlin, Truman Greene, Keith Harris, Wayne Ingle, Gene Phillips, and Ed Turner), for your sincere prayers and desire to see this project become a reality.

Dana and Joyce Abernathy, Steve and Kim Day, Clara Holly, Jeff and Julie Lanier, Greg Bliven, and Tunde Olutade, for caring about me during this journey. Your love and friendship have meant more than you will ever know.

Gene and Joann Crosby, for offering your wonderful, "quiet" Florida retreat so I could finish the revision.

The rest of my family, but especially my mother, Martha Graham, and Gary and Tammy Smith, for your tremendous love and counsel.

Sandy Smith, for bearing the burden of preparing so many revisions, keeping my office afloat while I worked on the book, and for "pestering" me to get the work done.

Vicki Crumpton, for fighting for this book and for the guidance, insight, and gentleness you graciously showed to such a rookie. I am very blessed that you became my editor.

Introduction

In 1979, after endless hours of studying, worrying, and pushing myself, I graduated from law school. The day was beautiful, the birds were singing, and graduation was everything I'd hoped it would be. My family was there, happy and proud, and all was right with the world.

Then I officially left the safety of the classroom and prepared for my introduction into the legal community. I can still remember the swearing-in ceremony, the crowded courtroom, the smiles, handshakes, and pats on the back. But nothing had prepared me for what I would discover.

During the next few months I became increasingly aware of something that most of the world took quite seriously: a genuine, sincere, and often heartfelt dislike for lawyers.

For a young man who had been taught the honor and nobility of the legal profession, this attitude came as quite a shock. The longer I practiced law, the more I understood why so much of its respect, honor, nobility, and dignity had been lost. While many lawyers worked hard to protect their clients and uphold their rights, others were lying, cheating, and using a system filled with loopholes for one purpose: to promote the financial interests of the lawyer.

For many, the legal profession had become the ultimate symbol of hypocrisy. Law firms, experts in fighting race and sex discrimination, used within their own halls a tradition-bound system of employment, promotion, and advancement that kept their ranks white and male. Environmental lawyers, who by day scorned ineffective agencies and battled polluting corporations, at night forged agreements to destroy projects that could bring water to people whose wells were rapidly running dry.

These lawyers talked a good game. But when it came to living up to the ideals they fought for, they fell short. Instead, they hid within a world they had created. No wonder people rejected them.

A few years later I had an even greater revelation. As before, it dealt with being a lawyer, but this time the attack came from within—and it struck at the very core of who I am.

It was 1984, and I was working on a case involving a dispute between two businessmen. The issue was serious in terms of the money involved, but both men were honorable and wanted what was right. Unfortunately what they saw as being *right* was filtered through their own biased eyes, preventing any meaningful discussion. To avoid a long and expensive lawsuit, I proposed to the other attorney that we use a third party as a mediator to resolve the misunderstandings on both sides. I had been a part of such efforts in church-related disputes and they were often successful. Since our clients were Christians, I believed this would be a good alternative.

After I described the process, there followed a long, uneasy silence. The other attorney finally said, in words I will remember for the rest of my life, "You are a disgrace to your profession for trying to be an attorney and a Christian at the same time."

I was stunned. Never had I considered the two as mutually exclusive. The only thing I could think to say was, "I take it you're not a Christian." He quickly responded, "I don't have time for my Sunday activities to get in the way of representing my clients."

As I've struggled with seeking to know and do God's will, I've often thought about that brief conversation and the philosophy of confining our Christianity to only one day or a few hours a week. Sadly, it's not only one man's lifestyle. You can find it in every corner of our "Christian society," and it endangers the true work of the church.

Discipleship stands awkwardly alone, lost in a sea of lukewarm belief that seeks to conform Christianity to the world's lifestyles and attitudes. The desire to follow Christ has been replaced with the desire simply to get along. We've become blind to the truth and don't know what we're doing or where we're headed.

It's long overdue for us as the children of God, the brothers and sisters of Christ, the heirs of the heavenly kingdom, to look long and hard at what we say we believe, show the world a life of truth, and not turn away from who we are and who we represent.

It is time to *take the stand*.

Charles B. Graham

I

The Lie
The False Witness

Pews will be packed today as most of the world's Christians celebrate the basis of their faith—the resurrection of Jesus. Some worshipers are new to the faith and sing out with the enthusiasm of new discovery. Some are occasional Christians who come only out of a sense of habit or obligation. Others are beginning a spiritual search that will lead to a new commitment to their faith. And some, who grew up singing Easter hymns, won't be there at all.

The Atlanta Journal, Easter Day, April 16, 1995

The Flickering Light

On New Year's Day 1984, another attorney and I formed a new law firm. For eight years, until we were led in different directions, our practice grew and helped many people. It also provided a wonderful way for us to grow as Christians.

Before we saw our first client, we put a great deal of thought into the purpose of our firm. We didn't want to be just two more "legal beagles" grinding out countless hours and burning the midnight oil. We had seen that world and wanted no part of it. Although we took our work seriously, the practice of law did not come first in our lives. We believed it was more important to spend time with our wives and watch our children grow.

At first our clients were few and the work was scarce. Eventually, we represented more than 1,000 individuals and businesses, including a few foreign companies. We faced many powerful opponents, and our work involved a broad spectrum of the law.

The primary goal of our venture, though, was that it be a Christian law firm. We didn't hang crosses in the windows or have a fish engraved on our letterhead. Although everyone must do as they feel led, I've always been a bit leery of such displays. We chose instead to let God's actions in our lives convey that we were Christians, always being ready to share our faith when the occasion arose.

Operating as a Christian law firm also opened a tremendous door of opportunity in the area of counseling. As we worked with our clients on their legal problems, we often counseled them about deeper troubles in their lives. God brought us people from all walks of life, all faiths and beliefs.

It was through such counseling that I first began to see the depth of a problem that is rapidly disrupting huge segments of the Christian community: *our failure as Christians to take a stand in this world and really live the life of a Christian.*

Behind the Façade

Several years ago, I counseled a lady who was going through an especially difficult time. Her name was Carol, and she lived in a small country town where most people knew each other. Her life seemed like the ideal many dream about. Her husband was a prominent businessman, highly respected in the community. She was a champion for the needy and homeless, working many hours in volunteer service that brought her public praise and recognition. She and her husband also had two beautiful children who were as highly regarded as their parents.

Carol and her family lived in one of the finest houses in town, swam in their own pool, and drove luxury cars. Their clothes were tailored and their jewelry was real. To top it off, they were pillars in their church. Carol sang in the choir and taught a women's Bible class. Her husband was a deacon and served on several committees. Even the children were active in many youth programs.

However, in the midst of this almost-fairy-tale existence, Carol faced secret burdens: Her marriage was failing, her family was disintegrating, and her life was falling apart. A dreadful emotion consumed her, the emotion of hatred—hatred for her husband, hatred for her children, hatred for her friends and family, hatred for her church, and hatred for herself.

As she walked me through her life, I became painfully aware that this family had fallen victim to the old lie that it was only necessary to act like a Christian at special times instead of actually being one all the time. Somehow their beliefs, dreams, relationships, and even their worship had become a false display for others to see. They had forgotten who they really were.

Many live behind such a façade, giving the appearance of Christian living without ever confronting the substance of the true Christian life. They become casual in their approach to God, instead of being committed to Him.

And so, when these "casual Christians," carelessly or by choice, live within this illusion, they discover that in the face of reality, they have no foundation at all. They turn to their faith and watch it disappear, for this is not real Christianity but only an image they have created.

Built on this façade, marriages fail, families break apart, friendships end, businesses close, and even ministries dissolve. People who were convinced of their own security find they have nothing to hold on to.

The decision not to live as a Christian in *all* areas of life has harmful consequences. The most immediate is the disruption of a meaningful and personal relationship with God. But because we are called to be examples of Christ to those around us, the consequences do not stop there. What one person may do will often directly affect someone he never even knew was watching.

Where Is the Light?

There is a story about a young pastor who visited an old man living across the street from his church. Every Sunday the old man sat on his front porch, drinking his coffee as he carefully watched the neatly dressed people enter through solid oak doors and disappear into the sanctuary beyond. He sat and watched, Sunday after Sunday.

Now the young pastor had recently come to this congregation and, making his rounds each Sunday morning, he would see this man sitting on his porch. The pastor asked several church members who the man was, but no one knew. In fact, few had ever noticed him.

So, bright and early one Sunday morning, the young pastor crossed the street, wearing his best smile and friendly demeanor. He passed the sidewalk and crossed the short distance to the porch. The old man sat there, never taking his eyes off this uninvited guest.

"Hey, how are you doing?" the pastor asked as he reached the steps.

There was a brief pause as though the old man was bothered at having to make the effort to speak. "Fine," he said curtly.

"I'm Dave Stewart, the new pastor across the street. I thought I might come by, introduce myself, and invite you to come worship with us."

The man said nothing.

The pastor, feeling a bit awkward, decided to talk about his church and began to describe its many activities, Bible studies, fellowships, and community service. Finally, again after no response, he asked, "Pardon me, sir, and I don't mean to pry, but are you a Christian?"

The old man put down his coffee and leaned forward.

"Yeah, I am. But you can stop your sales pitch right there. You're just wasting your time if you think you're going to get me in that church of yours. I won't be going. No, sir!"

The young pastor, shocked by this strong declaration, replied, "But if you're a child of God, why won't you come into His house?"

"Look for yourself," the man said as he stiffened with indignation. "See that man there? He's John Andrews, works at the bank. Three weeks ago he foreclosed on Mrs. Davis who lived down by the corner. She was three weeks late sending in her note payment. But, you see, that's prime commercial property the bank could use. And that woman over yonder. That's Linda Norris, the lady lawyer downtown. She represented that liquor store in the big zoning case last year. Threatened all the residents with a million dollar lawsuit if we opposed it coming in the neighborhood."

The young pastor listened patiently as the old man, with great disgust, named church member after church member and recounted their stories.

"No, sir," the man finally concluded. "I don't think I'll be coming. Your church is full of hypocrites."

After a brief pause, the pastor looked at the old man. "Well," he said as a smile slowly crossed his face, "one more won't hurt."

This story is frequently told among Christians, and it is quite telling on what we do. A sad reality and tragic commentary is passed off with a funny line or two. The storyteller, often a teacher or minister, will usually focus the message on the old man: his lack of understanding, his rebellion against God's church, or his sins. We are reminded to be careful when we reach back to throw that first stone.

Far too often we miss a crucial point. This old man was affected by what he saw in *Christians*. He formed opinions, strong opinions, about each of those people, about who they really were, not just who they appeared to be on any given Sunday. Ultimately, what he thought of individuals grew into an opinion of the entire congregation. For this man, what the church represented was simply the sum of the individual examples set by its members.

He saw church people acting one way and living another. He saw hypocrisy. He saw a life of lies. For him, the church became a house of liars, a façade. He saw people claiming to be God's children, and he was repulsed by the sight.

The Illusive Flame

If there's one thing we should learn from Carol's life and the story of the old man, it is this: *We are the vehicles through which others see Christ, and we are responsible for how they see Him.* They may be new Christians or members of a lost world, people we know intimately or strangers we pass on the street.

Some dispute the depth of this statement, arguing that before a person becomes a Christian, the Holy Spirit is already working in his heart, showing him the truth. Misconceptions, they claim, will not hinder a person's coming to Christ. Besides, those can be dealt with later.

How we try to dodge responsibility!

Being a true witness of Christ involves understanding that what we say and do directly affects the eternal lives of those around us. Being a true witness enables us to know the joy of leading someone to Christ and to feel the horror at seeing another headed for hell. Instead of insulating ourselves or searching to be comfortable in any given situation, we open our lives so others may see Christ. Jesus makes this clear. "'You are the light of the world. A city on a hill cannot be hidden. Neither do people light a lamp and put it under a bowl. Instead they put it on its stand, and it gives light to everyone in the house. In the same way, let your light shine before men, that they may see your good deeds and praise your Father in heaven'" (Matt. 5:14–16).

Why do we choose to follow certain passages in the Bible and ignore others? We can sit back and proclaim Jesus as our Savior, the Messiah, the Holy One of God, but still refuse to acknowledge our responsibility in the kingdom.

Many of us have developed *our* Christianity into an art form, but in this sense, it's an art of deception. In no other institution or endeavor do people so skillfully and without hesitation portray a role and take on an image while, at the same time, adamantly refusing to embody the truth which that image represents. We deceive others as to who we really are and evade responsibility for what we should be.

If we are the light of the world, we are at best a flickering flame, dancing from side to side, not offering a steady beam for those who are searching. Sadly, the light becomes illusive.

The degree to which Christians have failed to be Christ's light in this world has had catastrophic results. Christians are laughed at and scorned, some because of their faith and some because of their hypocrisy. Many of us are reluctant to let others know we are Christians because of what it could mean to our jobs, our relationships, or our influence. We might not get that promotion. We might lose some friends. People might stop taking us seriously.

And so, we become *careful*, not wanting to stir up any trouble. We seek that which makes us feel comfortable, even in how we handle our own Christianity, which for too many is only a shadow of the truth, a lukewarm religion in a hot and cold world . . . and a false witness.

What would it be like if your life were examined in a courtroom? What if Jesus were on trial and you were His only witness? For many, the transcript would read like this . . .

A Day in Court

"Oyez, oyez, oyez," the bailiff announces to the crowd. "All rise for the Honorable H. J. Lanier."

A robed figure quickly enters and sits behind a massive desk positioned high above the courtroom floor.

"Counselors," he begins, "I've reviewed your arguments concerning the testimony of the witness, and there has to be sufficient grounds to recall him for further questioning."

The defense attorney immediately steps forward. "Your Honor, he's already testified as to the facts in this case and as to his knowledge of my client. Any allegations of his own past conduct have no bearing here. The witness is not on trial. The issue at hand concerns my client, not whether the witness has been a perfect role model."

"But Your Honor," breaks in the prosecutor. "I completely agree that the issue is the guilt or innocence of the defendant. We've brought very serious charges against him, that for many years he's operated a scam, tricking innocent people into believing that he can make their lives better, when all along he just wanted to take away their rights and freedom. We've presented evidence that despite his claims that people would be loved and cared for, many have joined his organization only to be ignored and abused. He promised joy and peace, and they got only misery and torment. As a direct result of his lies, good men, women, and children have been led astray, losing their fortunes, their jobs, their friends . . . some even their lives.

"The defense has brought before this court a single witness to testify that his client can be trusted. This witness performed remarkably well, telling us of the defendant's love and kindness, that he treats his followers as his children and friends. He admitted the defendant boldly offers peace, joy, life without worry, and a host of other wonderful things to anyone who will just follow him. But most importantly, Your Honor, this witness said he personally knows the defendant and that what he claims is true . . . because the witness himself is a follower.

"May it please the court, we intend to present new evidence which will show a different side to this story. We will show, beyond any reasonable doubt, that the witness does not follow the defendant's teachings. We will show example after example in which the witness has failed to care for the elderly, neglected the homeless, ignored those in prisons, shunned people dying with AIDS or cancer, and refused to comfort the lonely, the grieving, and the despondent. We will paint a new picture of this witness, one of a self-centered, self-serving individual who does not hesitate to put his own interests first.

"And finally, Your Honor, we will show to everyone here a life in which, time after time, this witness has refused to acknowledge that he even knows the defendant."

The judge wearily rubbed his eyes and leaned back in his chair.

"Counselors, the witness's credibility is relevant to this case. Numerous claims of the defendant's character and abilities have been presented, and the only proof offered by the defense has been the testimony of this one person. If the prosecution can demonstrate that the witness has lied and is not a follower of the defendant, the court cannot rely on *any* statement he has made. If it is shown that the witness did not himself follow teachings which he claims are so important, his own actions can be used to demonstrate that the teachings have no merit.

"What we know of the defendant is based on the life of the witness. If the court cannot trust him, it is impossible for the court to trust anything the defendant has claimed to be true."

With a heavy sigh, the judge looked down at the prosecutor. "Call the witness."

The Conflict Within

We all dream of success. The problem, however, lies in how we define it.

During the Great Depression of the 1930s, if a man had a steady job, food for his family, and a house that provided warmth and shelter, he was considered both successful and fortunate. But today, success means more than having the necessities.

Years ago it was common for children to share a bedroom and think nothing of it. In fact, it may have helped them be closer as they grew older. Today, however, sharing a room is unthinkable. Believing the proper development of a child's personality requires that he have his own space, parents search for a house large enough to accommodate their growing family and borrow whatever it takes to get it. Necessities are only a small part of our new definition of success. We have decided we need more.

The Search for Satisfaction

We base success on our desires, ambitions, and motivations at particular times. We create and re-create this image of success on a daily basis. And then, just when we've figured out the game, the rules change.

Our desires, ambitions, and motivations also influence what we think of failure, quality of life, security, intelligence, loyalty, and morality. Ultimately, they affect everything involved in our perception of life, and they continually change it.

In the last fifty years, for example, we've seen the rapid dissolution of the institution of marriage. Today people often hope to make it through life with only one or two divorces. Although marriage was once held as a holy union, multiple marriages have become accepted as the norm in our society.

Premarital sex used to be strictly taboo. Unfortunately, it has not only become prevalent among teenagers, but it has also become the standard by which they and their parents often view growth and maturity. Yet they ignore the dramatic rise in teenage pregnancies and their devastating effect on young lives.

Desires, ambitions, and motivations change, and with them so do perceptions of right and wrong, good and bad, moral and immoral. Society makes new evaluations on the basis of two simple questions. The first is: Does it contribute to my personal satisfaction? The second is: What is necessary to achieve this satisfaction?

Notice I didn't say personal "happiness." Often a person will believe that the overall satisfaction of a given situation is of the utmost importance even though certain aspects of that situation may not make him or her particularly happy.

Consider the executive who *sacrifices* for his family. Early each morning he leaves for work where he will stay well into the evening. Work spills over into the weekend, making each day the same as the next. He seldom takes vacations because of the work and his need to be seen as diligent and hard working. Even when he takes time away with his family, he carries papers to review and reports to prepare.

He *sacrifices* so his family can live in a big house and his children can have the things he never had. And he tells himself that he really cares, even though he's never home long enough to tell anyone else. He may not be happy with his life, but he is satisfied. He is meeting his definitions of "success," "responsibility," "husband," and "father," definitions based on *personal* desires, ambitions, and motivations. Of course, he never asks his family about *their* desires.

People who follow this basis for living fool themselves. In pursuing their own satisfaction, they believe that they are seeking only what is reasonable or right, but they haven't taken the time to see how this pursuit ultimately changes them.

The end result of living by these two questions is the adoption of a dangerous attitude for life: The end justifies the means.

When our lives revolve around personal satisfaction, our happiness simply becomes the promotion of self. A great dilemma is then created, for even the newest Christian realizes that his faith somehow involves helping others, seeing to their needs, and putting self aside.

How does the average card-carrying Christian handle this situation? Not very well. Like Carol and those the old man had been watching, he hides behind a façade of Christianity, reserving his Christian walk for a few hours on Sunday. During that time he sings hymns, listens to a sermon, teaches others, and even serves on committees.

But once outside the confines of the building he calls his church, he quickly forgets who he is. He curses and uses God's name flippantly and in vain. He goes to work and plans how to place his enemies in a bad light while elevating himself. He chooses not to report all his income and claims deductions that never existed. He lies to cover up his failures, even when someone else must take the fall. He judges others and spreads stories he doesn't know to be true. He criticizes with no intent to encourage.

But there is something much worse. As is often the case, it isn't found in the commission of any particular act, but instead in the omission. The tragedy of his life is that he goes from day to day, moment to moment, never allowing even the slightest hint that he is Christian. He chooses to blend in and coexist, to get along without causing any trouble or commotion. He elects to be *a part* of this world, refusing to acknowledge that he is *apart* from it.

So the conflict rages. He adopts the world's view of happiness, security, satisfaction, and fairness, but the Holy Spirit within unsettles him. He tries to embrace the world with holy arms, yet finds no peace. He is left despondent, disillusioned, and confused.

A Difficult Journey

How many of us would pass up a life of luxury, with servants meeting our every whim, for a life of drudgery and backbreaking labor? Or who would choose to live in poverty, with no running water or electricity, instead of the comforts of a modern suburban home?

As a matter of fact, we are taught that there can only be one rational choice in such instances. We may cite examples such as Mother Teresa and Dr. David Livingston, but we immediately label these people as either saints or eccentrics. They certainly are not normal or on a level to which we could aspire. They are different from the rest of us. If they do represent virtue, it is only for certain special people, not for us. Such a life would be too difficult.

By making such arguments, we calm any fears we might have about our own inadequacies. We can then go along with the *ordinary* people without feeling the least bit guilty. Since our natural tendency is to seek our own satisfaction, what we're really doing is simply looking out for "number one," usually taking the easiest path to get where we want to be. And if we claim to be Christian, this can present an uncomfortable problem when God calls us to take the narrow road.

I paid for most of my college education by working for a public utility company. Whether it was raining or sunny, a hundred degrees or five below, I would get my assignment and spend the day walking from house to house, reading hundreds of meters and sometimes collecting overdue bills.

I always find it interesting when people tell me how much my education must mean to me because I worked for it. "You really know the value of a good education," they report. With few exceptions, these people either didn't go to college or had their way paid for them. They didn't miss out on spring trips to the beach or beg off from going out to dinner because they barely had enough money to make their own meals. But for all their kind remarks, they simply don't know what they're talking about.

Now don't misunderstand. I greatly appreciated my job and the fact that I was able to go to college. Many others had it far worse than I did. But truth be told, I would rather have had it easier. When people say I was fortunate to learn the value of my education, I quickly tell them I figured that out early on. I really didn't need the extra years of hard work to drive the point home.

It is seldom fun to take the difficult road or the hardest way. *But that's the reality for a Christian!* Jesus said: "'Enter through the narrow gate. For wide is the gate and broad is the road that leads to destruction, and many enter through it. But small is the gate and narrow the road that leads to life, and only a few find it'" (Matt. 7:13–14).

The journey for the Christian is often a difficult one, filled with hardship and heartache. Jesus warns us to expect this. We will be oppressed and ridiculed. Why? Simply because we follow Him.

Yet we seldom understand, usually because we are caught up in the world's vision of success and satisfaction. Just look at many of the hymns we sing every Sunday. They tell of having Jesus as Savior and finding eternal joy, happiness, and peace, but we mistakenly translate these to mean not having another care. We take the message of the gospel and read it with the eyes of the world.

For instance, take John 3:16, often used as the foundation for a person's belief that he or she is a Christian. How many times have you heard someone say, "I know I'm saved because I believe that Jesus is the Son of God," and then he recites John 3:16? Sadly, a critical point has been ignored. "'For God so loved the world that he gave his one and only son, that whoever believes in him shall not perish but have eternal life.'"

Many read this so quickly that they believe all they have to do is acknowledge who Jesus is, and then they are miraculously saved and can call themselves Christian. But the key here is found in the phrase *believes in*.

There are many things we believe to exist, but far fewer we believe in. For example, there is no doubt that abortions occur every day. This is a fact supported by documented evidence, and we believe such information to be true. However, it is an entirely different matter to say we *believe in* abortion.

To *believe in* something requires not only that we accept its existence but also that we claim it for ourselves, allowing it to be a part of our thoughts and actions. It becomes a part of who we are. When an individual believes in Jesus as the Son of God, the teachings, commands, and example of Christ become an integral part of his life. They are adopted as his own. He becomes a student dedicated to being like the Teacher.

Believing in Jesus is more than just acknowledging an existence. It's a commitment.

The very definition of the word *Christian* should tell us this. To be Christian means to be Christlike, a follower of Christ. Yet so many fail to understand the words. They try to manufacture their own salvation, defining the Christian life in terms of what they are comfortable with . . . an easy road that's not too demanding. In short, they compromise.

The Great Compromise

As a negotiator, I am well aware of the nature of impasses. Opposing sides fear they may lose ground or provide the other with some real or imagined advantage. Frustration sets in, emotions rise, and battle lines are drawn. In other words, they refuse to budge.

The goal of a negotiator is to find some common ground through which he can develop a plan for both sides to win, where everyone gets something without feeling they've just given away the farm. It's often tricky work, requiring hours of studying the desires of both sides. But by concentrating on how each party can gain, a compromise is usually found and everyone can go home happy.

In the same way, we sometimes seek a compromise in our Christian beliefs so that we too can go home happy. In so doing, we undermine the very foundation of our witness to the world, not to mention our own belief in who we are and who God is.

This great compromise develops through one of three paths or attitudes. *The first and foremost is our failure, if not outright refusal, to take the time to understand what our beliefs are.*

For Christians our primary resources are the Bible and prayer, but how often do we really study God's Word or pray? For many, the times are few and far between, and there's always a ready excuse. "I've had to work a lot lately." "The kids were impossible today." "I just had to take some time for myself."

How hard is it, though, to find time for that special TV show or ball game? What about those few hours shopping at the store or reading the paper? And what about that week of vacation? We always seem to find the time when we're interested in our own satisfaction. Are we really more concerned with cutting the grass, cleaning the house, or walking the dog than in spending time with Him? We may give God an appointment in our lives, but then *we* don't show up.

If we don't study the Bible or pray as we should, we can't be enlightened by God's Holy Spirit. We will remain confused and travel the wrong way. We may do the best we can by ourselves, but ultimately we change God's commands, directions, and guidance for our lives to make them compatible with the expectations of the world.

Sadly, we're satisfied with this distortion, convincing ourselves that we've done an admirable job. "After all, who has time to study? We still have a life to live. If God wants us to let others see how good we are, surely He can't expect us to spend so much time reading and discussing His Word. Besides, we're smart enough and can figure it out on our own."

Yet throughout the Bible, Jesus never refers to His followers as students who are "fully trained." There's always the need for more work. Unfortunately, we act as though we expect to be filled with complete understanding and wisdom the instant we become a Christian. We fail to seek the higher understanding which comes only from God. So, without realizing it, we begin to compromise.

The second way we compromise our beliefs is by trying to substitute our common sense for the will of God. Of course, we don't call it that. Instead, we refer to such compromises as interpretations.

For example, two men get into a bitter argument over a financial issue in their church, resulting in some hard feelings. To avoid further arguing, they leave soon after a business meeting. Separately, they decide to avoid each other for several weeks to "let things simmer down."

The problem with this common sense approach is that it directly violates Jesus' commands about disputes among Christians. When Jesus gives a command, there's nothing left to discuss. Yet in our *finite* wisdom, we somehow believe we have the right to alter His commands in any given situation, as if Jesus could not possibly have foreseen this particular event.

The last method by which we compromise our beliefs is simply through treating God's Word as though it never existed. We choose to ignore anything that doesn't meet with our satisfaction. If God's law interferes with what we want, we pretend that it is not there "just this one time."

We can see this in many people who are in business for themselves and use the common practice of bartering. Instead of paying for something, they simply swap different products or services. However, many use this as a way to avoid paying income taxes and fail to report the bartered item or service as compensation.

God's Word is very clear. Jesus specifically directs us to pay our taxes. If we refuse, we steal from the government and break one of God's commands. But personal comfort and satisfaction can take on greater importance than following God. So we choose to ignore Him and His commands.

Compromising our beliefs affects everything we do and everything we claim to be. It allows us to make life a bit easier, the gate a bit wider, and the road a bit broader. Unlike compromises in business, though, a compromise between us and God leaves only one side satisfied, and even that is temporary.

As we continue to compromise, we become oblivious to its destructiveness as well as to our growing complacency toward God. Yet we shake our heads as the world pulls further from Him, and we don't understand that we carry a lot of the blame.

Back to the Basics

Our attitudes and beliefs affect everything around us. They even affect the image of Christianity we project. To present the true witness of Christ, we must come to terms with these attitudes and beliefs, test them against God's Word, and align them with His will. In doing so, it's important that we study our interactions with other people, for that is where our witness is expressed.

Four areas of interaction are especially critical to our understanding of how to be true Christian witnesses. These are the home, the workplace, the church, and the community. In the final segment of this book we will discuss the effects a false witness of Christ has in these areas as well as look at practical things we can do to get back on track.

So far we've stated the problem of the false witness in this way: Many of us have become casual Christians, relegating our Christian conduct primarily to certain special times, while otherwise adopting a lifestyle that at best projects a façade of Christianity which embraces the desires, ambitions, and motivations of the world.

How has this happened? Why do we sometimes fail to act like Christians or let others know who we are?

The key to any problem is understanding its cause. Consider an issue in many churches: A Bible study class doesn't reach out to visitors. It becomes stagnant in numbers and spiritual growth; it doesn't interact well with the rest of the church or become involved in the church's community mission work.

Many churches try to solve the problem by treating the symptoms. They promote "visitation night" to call on anyone who has an interest in the church; they hold contests to see who can get the most visitors; and when all else fails, they use guilt to get their members involved. These methods seldom work because they don't go to the cause.

One class, however, decided to focus on the heart of their problem, and what they discovered was interesting.

Although they were asking members to reach out to visitors, they weren't encouraging or caring for each other. They asked themselves, "How can we show love and concern for strangers when we're not doing the same for our friends?" The answer was simple: They couldn't. Armed with this insight, they began to teach the importance of caring for one another and *setting an example for others to see*. Once they were showing their love for people they knew, it was easier and more natural for them to reach out to visitors.

What is important here is that the class met the challenge. They got back to basics and worked to resolve the cause of their problem. In turn, they provided a basis for the witness they were to have in their community.

We too can use this method of focusing on the cause to understand the problem created by casual Christians, and then work to resolve it. We don't have to be discouraged or shake our heads in defeat.

We can have a deeper commitment to acting like Christians when we get back to the basics—acknowledging who God really is and who we are in relation to Him. This is where the cause of the problem lies. Our first task then is to determine, as best we can, who God is.

II

The Truth
Who Is God?

The fear of the LORD is the beginning of wisdom,
and knowledge of the Holy One is understanding.

Proverbs 9:10

THREE

The Otherness
of God

When we don't understand who God is, we develop a distorted perception of the world and of our place in it. If we look only to one aspect of God's entire character, we fail to appreciate the depth of His commands and teachings.

During the early history of this country, religion took on a very strict, puritan flavor. Sermons generally centered on God's wrath, His divine judgment for sinners, and His punishment through eternal damnation for those too foolish to repent. Today we call these "fire and brimstone" sermons. Their effectiveness was based on the degree of guilt, shame, and fear they could arouse within the poor soul sitting in the pew. Although many responded to these sermons, their strength began to fade. People were being introduced to only one side of God's character. They didn't know of His tremendous love, gentleness, joy, patience, or peace. All they heard were the negative orations depicting an angry God.

The last fifty years have seen a great change. Sermons slowly have shifted from the day of judgment to a life of love. We are no longer reminded of responsibilities and our call to obedience. Instead, we are taught only to love each other as Christ loved us and to strive toward the fruits of the Spirit.

Unfortunately, we have merely experienced the swinging of a pendulum. For just as it went too far in one direction, it has since traveled too far in the other. At first we ignored God's love, grace, and mercy. Now we fail to understand God's wrath and His requirement that we be committed to Him.

What we need is a balanced view of God. Instead of a pendulum subject to our influence, we should see a scale where all of God's attributes are weighed out in perfect harmony. This would mean accepting that He dispenses discipline and love at the same time; He issues punishment and mercy; He both loves and hates—all in a perfect balance.

Holy, Holy, Holy

Who is God? The Book of Revelation provides the answer. Four creatures surrounding God's heavenly throne call out: "Holy, holy, holy is the Lord God Almighty, who was, and is, and is to come" (Rev. 4:8b).

Day and night, they proclaim this message for all to hear, and through it, they praise God for who He is, three times describing Him as holy.

What does it mean to be holy? It means to be set apart; characterized by perfection and transcendence; commanding absolute adoration and awe; spiritually pure; being awesome, frightening, or beyond belief. If we are to understand who God is, it is essential that we seek to know what is meant when the Bible says He is "holy, holy, holy."

Complete

First, recall that the living creatures in Revelation 4:8 refer to God as being holy three times. This is very significant. When the Bible was written, a certain style was used to show special emphasis or importance.

Frequently in the Books of Matthew, Mark, Luke, and John, as translated in the King James Version, Jesus begins an instruction by saying, "Verily, verily." Today's translations will often begin those same passages by the phrase, "I tell you the truth." While this properly translates the word *verily*, it loses the emphasis Jesus was giving. To be more exact, we should see, "I tell you the truth, I tell you the truth."

The key is that Jesus begins by saying the word or words twice. To the listener in Jesus' time, that would be the same as if Jesus had said, "Now listen carefully to what I'm about to say because it is very important." By stating something twice, the Speaker was indicating a degree of importance.

But in Revelation, the living creatures cry out that God is holy not once or twice, but three times. In that culture repeating anything three times gave it the utmost importance, making it complete in whatever it might be.

Here we find the proclamation that God is "holy, holy, holy." The creatures were shouting that God is completely holy, that He is purely holy, and there is nothing more holy than the Lord God Almighty. The Bible refers to many places and objects as holy, but God and God alone is ever described in this all-encompassing way.

Beyond and Apart

When I was growing up, I had what I thought were very important questions about why God did the things He did. One day I mentioned these to one of the older men in my church. After I described my questions and earnest desire to understand, the man smiled and told me, "Well, the way I see it, it's like this: God never showed the whole plan or all of His deepest secrets to Abraham, Moses, Elijah, or even Solomon. He never shared everything with Peter or Paul, James or John. So what about *you* is so special that He would feel the need to share it all with you?"

Needless to say, that wasn't the answer I was looking for. As I recall, my elaborate comeback was a weak, "Yeah, but . . ."

As we grow spiritually, drawing closer to God and knowing Him better, it's best to remember that there will be certain things which are simply beyond our human understanding. Try as we might, we cannot grasp the fullest meaning. Take the time before creation when there was nothing. How do we comprehend that? And what about a power that can create something out of nothing simply by speaking? It's beyond our ability to understand.

In the same way, it's difficult to understand God's holiness, for it's this aspect of His nature that sends everything into the superlative—abounding love, grace greater than all our sins, burning and eternal hatred for evil, absolute purity, and righteousness. We understand to a point, but can then go no further.

I met a man who served in a special missions unit during the Vietnam War. He described horrible acts of the Vietcong never reported on the evening news. He also told how he personally carried out orders in committing equally horrible atrocities for the good side. After an emotional outpouring, he said simply, "I'll never understand how God could have forgiven me for what I did."

Some things we can't understand. Some things we were not meant to understand. We just have to accept them, live on faith, and move on.

God's holiness is greater than our ability to understand. The depth and extent of God's love and hate, His grace and punishment, and His mercy and judgment are too much for us to comprehend. R. C. Sproul in his book, *The Holiness of God,* refers to God's nature as His "otherness." God is holy. He is set apart. He is pure and very unlike mankind. He is infinite; we are finite. God is other. He is beyond all we could ever possibly imagine.

The Book of Isaiah gives a vivid account of what happens when we approach that holy Presence. Isaiah was a respected priest, widely known in the kingdom. He was also a statesman and had immediate access to the royal courts. He was by all accounts the most righteous man in the realm. Then one day he went to the temple and had a vision that changed everything he ever thought about God and about himself. In that vision, he witnessed magnificence and majesty. He saw power and authority. He beheld a holy God.

As he watched, mighty seraphs, like the living creatures in Revelation, flew and called to one another: "'Holy, holy, holy is the LORD Almighty; the whole earth is full of his glory.' At the sound of their voices the doorposts and thresholds shook and the temple was filled with smoke" (Isa. 6:3b–4).

But more important than the elaborate description of this unusual scene is what happened to Isaiah when he found himself in the presence of God. "'Woe to me!' I cried. 'I am ruined!'" (Isa. 6:5a).

Now here was a man of God and a devoted servant. He was righteous before the Lord, respected, and honored. There was no one like him in the kingdom. Yet when this same man came into the presence of God's holiness, he immediately cried out that he was doomed and utterly undone. Though he was great before men, Isaiah discovered he was nothing in the presence of God. His human goodness faded completely when compared to the pure goodness of the Lord. His earthly righteousness vanished before the righteousness of a holy God.

God's holiness is great and awesome, going far beyond the limits of what we can imagine. As Isaiah found, we could not bear to be in the presence of His holiness. We would see ourselves for what we really are, and the truth of how far we are from God would completely destroy us.

As we gain a better understanding of who God is, we find that He is separate and apart from anything we've ever known. He is all-powerful and all-knowing. He is always present, regardless of where we may be. And He has such a depth of love, mercy, and kindness that we stand amazed.

Most importantly, we come to know that God is holy, holy, holy. He is awesome, evoking respect and fear, love and obedience. Only when we have this growing knowledge of God can we begin to understand who we are in relation to Him.

Seeing more clearly who God is and what He has done in our lives will create within us a desire to be the people He wants us to be. This desire will grow into a heartfelt commitment through which we will show others a true witness of Christ and a better way.

"I Am Who I Am"

Although we may feel lonely at times, even depressed and abandoned, God never hides from us. Through all the centuries, as we've advanced from cavemen to nuclear scientists, God has always been with us. He hasn't changed in any way. He is consistent.

Because it is difficult to explain something beyond our comprehension, we can get a better idea of who God is by looking at what we do understand, such as power, knowledge, space, and time. Using these as guides, we have come to describe God as omnipotent (all-powerful), omniscient (all-knowing), and omnipresent (always present).

God Is All-Powerful

The Bible contains many examples of God's awesome power: the devastation of the great flood, the parting of the Red Sea, the sending of plagues, and even the raising of the dead. And while these amazed us as children, I fear they have taken a back seat to the "miracles" we have created.

For example, God parted the Red Sea, but look at the river diversion projects and massive dams we have engineered. Certainly Lazarus was brought back to life, but how often do we hear of doctors *healing* the sick, surgeons *reviving* a stopped heart, and medicine *saving* lives? We see images on boxes called televisions, and jets let us fly. A switch brings light to our world. We have many amazing devices, gadgets, and toys for our comfort, health, and entertainment. And as we take pride in our accomplishments, God's miracles pale in comparison.

There is one demonstration of God's power, however, for which there is no comparison . . . the miracle of creation. "In the beginning God created the heavens and the earth. Now the earth was formless and empty, darkness was over the surface of the deep, and the Spirit of God was hovering over the waters. And God said, 'Let there be . . . '" (Gen. 1:1–3a).

God has such incredible power that all He has to do is speak and something is created. No laboratory or experiments. No trainloads of raw material. He simply utters a word and mountains form, seas swell, rain falls, and wind blows. From absolute nothing to full existence. Now that's power!

People in the military understand this kind of authority. When a general gives an order, it's carried out with no question or hesitation. He doesn't ask or plead, nor is it necessary to shout out the command. His voice is enough. A soldier understands and obeys.

God's authority works much the same way. Once when Jesus was crossing the Sea of Galilee, a violent storm suddenly came. Seeing that His disciples were frightened, He spoke to the wind and the waves, saying, "'Quiet! Be still!'" Immediately the wind died down and the sea was calm (see Mark 4:35–39). *Nature responded to the sound of His voice!* God's power is so awesome that even the wind and the water obey.

The Bible doesn't say that Jesus shouted in a loud voice or that there were thunder and lightning when He spoke. Sometimes we portray biblical events in a grander style, as though that were necessary for us to believe. In so doing, we miss something very important in our understanding of who God is, something even Elijah once failed to see.

Here was a great prophet who challenged the followers of Baal on Mount Carmel. He told them to prepare two bulls on a stack of wood and then pray for the wood to be lit. "'The god who answers by fire—he is God'" (1 Kings 18:24b). Although they shouted and cried, the prophets of Baal received no answer. Their god remained silent.

Elijah prepared his altar, arranging twelve stones to represent the tribes of Jacob. He cut the bull into pieces and placed them on the wood. Finally, he dug a trench around the altar, filled it with water, and poured water on the wood three times. Then he prayed. "'Answer me, O Lord, answer me, so these people will know that you, O Lord, are God. . . .' Then the fire of the Lord fell and burned up the sacrifice, the wood, the stones and the soil, and also licked up the water in the trench" (1 Kings 18:37–38).

Amazing! Awesome! Surely this is what it means when we say God is all-powerful. Right? But look a little further.

In the days that followed, a price was put on Elijah's head. Because of what happened at Mount Carmel, all of the queen's prophets had been killed and she was disgraced. For this, she wanted Elijah dead.

Did Elijah turn to God for comfort? Did he rest in the assurance of an all-powerful God? No. He ran away. Frightened by the power of this queen, he panicked and fled.

Elijah had fallen into a trap we also find ourselves in from time to time. When a crisis occurs, we're quick to call on "the God who answers by fire." For us, His power is demonstrated by grand, dynamic, and immediate occurrences of unexplainable phenomena. If what results is not grand, dynamic, or immediate, and especially if it can be explained by natural causes, we begin to doubt God's power as well as our belief in the God we thought we knew. But look closely at the rest of the story.

> And the word of the LORD came to him: "What are you doing here, Elijah?" He replied, ". . . I am the only one left, and now they are trying to kill me too." The LORD said, "Go out and stand on the mountain in the presence of the LORD, for the LORD is about to pass by." Then a great and powerful wind tore the mountains apart and shattered the rocks before the LORD, but the LORD was not in the wind. After the wind there was an earthquake, but the LORD was not in the earthquake. After the earthquake came a fire, but the LORD was not in the fire. And after the fire came a gentle whisper. When Elijah heard it, he pulled his cloak over his face and went out and stood at the mouth of the cave. (1 Kings 19:9b–13a)

What Elijah learned was that while God may express Himself through fire, storms, furious wind, and earthquakes, He doesn't have to depend on such grand displays. Instead, His power is such that He can summon a gentle whisper from nothing and use it to speak to His people.

The French philosopher René Descartes once said, "I think, therefore I am." But he wasn't saying that his thoughts caused his existence, only that they were proof of it.

God, on the other hand, tells us, "I speak, and therefore you are." Our existence as well as the existence of all things is due directly to His power, which is truly awesome and demands respect and honor. Although we play with genetics and attempt to "create" life, we can't come close to what God can do. God is the embodiment of power, and He alone has the authority.

God Is All-Knowing

Of all the blessings God has so graciously given me, and the number is far too great to count, among the greatest is my wife. Beverly and I have known each other most of our lives. We began dating when we were sixteen. In fact, she's the only girl I ever dated. We waited seven years before we were married, and since then have had three wonderful children.

We have shared each other's pains and sorrows as well as our joys and celebrations. We've struggled together, succeeded together, feared together, laughed together, cried together, and prayed together. We talk to each other and we listen. And our love has grown far beyond what we thought it could ever be.

In all of this time and through all our adventures, we have come to know each other quite well. I don't need to hear her voice to know she's worried. I don't have to tell her when I'm down. We just know. But what we know is still based on what we perceive. This may be from actions as well as inaction. It may come from the way we hold our heads, the look on our faces, or some faraway stare.

When we say that God is all-knowing, we mean something entirely different. God knows who we are and what lies within our hearts. He sees the ideas that fill our heads and feels the emotion within our soul. He knows every thought, concern, care, and feeling. He knows everything! "The LORD does not look at the things man looks at. Man looks at the outward appearance, but the LORD looks at the heart'" (1 Sam. 16:7b).

One aspect of God's knowledge is critical for us to grasp if we're to better understand who He is. When the Bible says "the LORD looks at the heart," it means that God knows our hidden motives in all situations, "'for the LORD searches every heart and understands every motive behind the thoughts'" (1 Chron. 28:9b).

He not only sees what we do and how we feel, but He also knows why we act a certain way or say a certain thing. We may fool those around us or even deceive ourselves, but we can't fool or deceive God. He knows.

As if that were not enough, God's knowledge transcends time. He not only knows everything that has ever occurred and all that is happening now, but also everything that is yet to come. The closest we get to knowing the future is when we try to create it by manipulating the present. But despite our best attempts, we don't have that kind of knowledge.

As we come to grips with who God is, we have to admit that there is a depth of knowledge—God's knowledge—that we will never have.

The psalmist put it best when he wrote: "O LORD, you have searched me and you know me. You know when I sit and when I rise; you perceive my thoughts from afar. You discern my going out and my lying down; you are familiar with all my ways. Before a word is on my tongue you know it completely, O LORD. You hem me in, behind and before; you have laid your hand upon me. Such knowledge is too wonderful for me, too lofty for me to attain" (Ps. 139:1–6).

God alone is the one "who was, and is, and is to come." He knows each and every time we violate His will. And He knows when our witness is a lie.

God Is Always Present

James Taylor once recorded a popular song entitled "You've Got a Friend." It spoke of a deep friendship that would survive the rough times. Through the simple words and soft melody, he reminded us of what it means to have someone we can count on. God is like that kind of friend—only better. He's *always* there! We can count on Him.

Sometimes we find this hard to believe, especially when we feel lonely and abandoned. Although we've been taught that God will always be with us, such feelings are natural and come quickly when we focus on ourselves, when the pain and depression seem too great to bear.

Some have argued that God is not always present, that He does abandon His children from time to time. They point to Jesus' words during the crucifixion as proof. "About the ninth hour Jesus cried out in a loud voice, *'Eloi, Eloi, lama sabachthani?'*—which means, 'My God, my God, why have you forsaken me?'" (Matt. 27:46).

They fail to understand that this passage supports rather than detracts from our claim that God is always with us. Jesus' message was not in the particular words He used, but in what they represented, for these words were the beginning of a passage of Scripture every devout Jew would have recognized: Psalm 22.

This psalm of David tells us two things. First, it describes the actual crucifixion Jesus was forced to suffer. By repeating the beginning of this familiar passage, Jesus was giving God's people one more chance to see who He really is.

Second, He was telling each and every one of us that He knows what it's like to suffer. He knows real pain and especially how it feels when you think you're all alone, abandoned, and forsaken. But He also tells us more, for the psalm doesn't end in dejected loneliness.

Instead, it concludes with praise to God and commitment to further-ing His kingdom. "You who fear the LORD, praise him! All you de-scendants of Jacob, honor him! Revere him, all you descendants of Israel! For he has not despised or disdained the suffering of the af-flicted one; he has not hidden his face from him but has listened to his cry for help" (Ps. 22:23–24).

Jesus' message is simple: In times of suffering and loss, even though we may feel alone and abandoned, God is still here. We can't trust our feel-ings. We have to trust Him. He has not left us alone, for God is *always* present.

After the crucifixion, the disciples felt great sorrow, anxiety, and lone-liness. Jesus took care of their immediate concerns when He returned, but He knew He would not be staying with them in His human form. It was important for His disciples to understand that He was not a Christ who was there only when they were dejected. So in the final days before His as-cension into heaven, Jesus shared with His friends the greatest comfort they would have as they traveled through the world telling others of the good news. "'All authority in heaven and on earth has been given to me. Therefore go and make disciples of all nations, baptizing them in the name of the Father and of the Son and of the Holy Spirit, and teaching them to obey everything that I have commanded you. *And surely I am with you always, to the very end of the age*'" (Matt. 28:18b–20, emphasis added).

God is with us always. He is with us in all His power, and He is with us in all His knowledge. Always.

In this chapter, we've just begun to see who God is. To really get to know Him, we have to spend time with Him. This is no different from any other relationship. We never really know another person unless we speak with him, hear what he believes, and how he feels about things. In other words, it's necessary to have an intimate time of sharing.

It is exactly the same with God. We study His Word, pray, and share our experiences with other Christians so that we can understand more from them. And God has promised that if we do, He will make Himself known to us. "Come near to God and he will come near to you" (James 4:8a).

❧

A Matter of Idolatry

Sometimes good people, who fill the pews on Sunday morning and even provide leadership in the church, actually honor a god of their own making. The Bible calls this idolatry.

Idolatry can occur in several ways: (1) giving anything priority over God, (2) believing Him to be something He's not, and (3) choosing what parts of the Bible to believe. None require a secret ritual for worshiping golden images, but the result is the same: We are concentrating on something else.

Hidden Idolatry

Putting anything ahead of God makes it the object of our attention and the focus of our concern. This form of idolatry is often found in church work, hidden behind good intentions.

For example, consider these two functions carried out in many churches on Sunday morning: keeping the records and counting the offerings. Good church records show which members were present, which were absent, the guests in attendance, and so forth. However, this work is frequently done during the time set aside for Bible study. While many are learning more about God and who they are as Christians, others gather statistical data, make calculations, and prepare nicely printed reports.

Some churches count offerings during the worship hour. Instead of attending that special service in which we come together to worship

God, sing praises to His name, and hear instruction from His Word, some choose to count the weekly contributions. Isn't this attention to money one of the desecrations of God's house that Jesus denounced? Wasn't He so upset that He flew into a rage, turning over tables and benches? Didn't He say that of all things concerning God's house, it is to be a house of prayer?

Both of these examples send a subtle, yet false, message: Spending time with God, through studying His Word or worshiping Him, can be less important than an administrative function.

It is easy to put something ahead of God. Those who keep records or count money would deny that they are giving those duties such priority. But more important than our words are our actions, for they demonstrate whether our words have any meaning.

Remember James' warning about our claim of faith: "Faith by itself, if it is not accompanied by action, is dead" (James 2:17), and again, "I will show you my faith by what I do" (James 2:18). If we act differently from what we claim with our mouths, then our words become lies and our witness useless.

Putting something ahead of God gives priority to that object or activity. It may be counting money or keeping records, a building program or a church bus, a youth camp or a senior adult trip. When it becomes the priority in our lives, we worship it as though it were our golden calf on the altar. "'You shall have no other gods before me. You shall not make for yourself an idol in the form of anything in heaven above or on the earth beneath or in the waters below. You shall not bow down to them or worship them; for I, the LORD your God, am a jealous God'" (Exod. 20:3–5a).

If we are to know Him, then we must understand this about God: He alone is to have priority in our lives, and we are not to allow anything to interfere with that status.

God Made to Order

There were once two ladies, Nancy and Beth, who were said to be Christians. Each attended her own church regularly and taught children in Sunday School. One of the passages they memorized with the children was 1 John 4:8: "Whoever does not love does not know God, because God is love."

"God is love" became the focus of all their teachings. It also became the foundation for all of their beliefs.

Though their lives were very similar, everything changed in 1941. With the coming of World War II, Nancy joined the Army as a nurse and served in the Philippines, giving medical attention to thousands of innocent natives injured in the conflict. Beth stayed home, helping those whose loved ones had gone to war and giving comfort when the news came that they would not be coming home. Through it all, Nancy and Beth often thought back to the times when they taught the children that "God is love."

I met these ladies in the last years of their lives, and I found it amazing how two individuals could start out so much alike and end up being so different. Though they didn't know each other, they suffered from the same problem. Neither one had an understanding of who God really is.

In spite of what Nancy took to the Philippines, she didn't return with the belief that God is love. In fact, she no longer believed in God at all. She once explained that all her life she had been taught and had taught others that God is love, but the war changed all that. Nancy reasoned that if God were truly a god of love, He would never have allowed the atrocities she witnessed. She felt that when people most needed God, He wasn't there. A god of love would never have abandoned people like that. Nancy died a lonely and bitter woman.

Beth, on the other hand, fell out of touch with God, but in a completely different way. She truly believed that God is love, but she also believed that He is nothing but love. See the difference?

She became interested in *good* people and their *good* causes, supporting movements for human rights, the environment, cancer research, the homeless, and many other efforts to better the world in which we live. She would see "God's love" working in the lives of atheists and agnostics, Hindus and Moslems, those who believe God is a force that is in everything and those who believe that everyone is a part of a force they call God.

She never considered witnessing to these *good* people, for in her mind, there was no need. If God is love, how could He possibly send a soul, who had done so much *good*, to eternal hell? She finally reasoned that He could not and would not. Why? Because God is love and He loves us all.

Both women started with the same belief and each ended quite differently. They simply did what many Christians do without ever realizing it. They created their own god. Taking hold of only one part of His character, Nancy and Beth each formed a supreme being that was nothing but love, ignoring everything else. They believed Him to be something He is not; consequently, they never really understood who God is.

Selective Bible Study

Nancy's and Beth's idolatry began when they followed their own desires of what they wanted God to be. Idolatry can also result when we choose to accept certain parts of the Bible while ignoring others. God's message of who He is becomes distorted, and we are easily led to worship a god that doesn't exist. This can occur especially when we consider such attributes as the nature of His love.

The Bible, of course, tells us that God is love and that the depth of His love is enormous. Regardless of how hard we try, we cannot grasp a complete understanding of His love and all that flows from it. But at the same time, God's Word reminds us repeatedly that He has anger, hatred, and jealousy as well as joy, gentleness, and kindness. He has abundant grace and mercy, but He also disciplines and bears eternal judgment.

And He is consistent. The Bible clearly shows us that since time began, God has been the same. He's never changed. The mercy and love He has for us now, He first showed to Adam and Eve in the Garden of Eden. The hatred He has for evil, He has demonstrated from the first.

God's presence does not mean there will be automatic love and peace in our lives. In fact, Jesus warned us that just the opposite will be true. "'Do not suppose that I have come to bring to the earth. I did not come to bring peace, but a sword. For I have come to turn "a man against his father, a daughter against her mother, a daughter-in-law against her mother-in-law—a man's enemies will be the members of his own household"'" (Matt. 10:34–36).

God is love, but He brings enormous *tension* to our lives because the world does not love Him. Nonetheless it is our responsibility to tell what the world does not want to hear and refuses to accept. The good news is not always accepted with open arms and smiling faces.

God's love is not what Nancy and Beth believed it to be or hoped it would become. It isn't some eternal warm, fuzzy feeling that God has for all living creatures. His love is not an emotion at all. Jesus described the nature of His love in the Book of John. "'Whoever has my commands and obeys them, he is the one who loves me'" (John 14:21a).

The love between God and His people is defined in terms of obedience. If we want to remain in God's love, we must obey His commands. On the other hand, when we choose to violate His commands and not follow the life of Christ, we have no right to expect that we will be in God's love. John drives this home when he tells us: "But if anyone obeys his word, God's love is truly made complete in him. This is how we know we are in him: Whoever claims to live in him must walk as Jesus did" (1 John 2:5–6).

The love we are to have for one another can be seen in our actions of sacrifice. When we care for the welfare of others and do something for them, we demonstrate God's love, *but only a portion of it.*

This is where many form their own god. Nancy and Beth believed that God is love, but it was a love defined in terms of human effort, in other words, in the way we help each other physically.

Jesus placed no such restrictions on His love. He simply said, "Love one another." People like Nancy and Beth change this instruction to mean an emotionally charged expression of concern for the physical well-being of humanity with little or no regard for *spiritual* well-being.

They fail to understand that God's love encompasses far more. His love has been expressed through the birth, life, and death of His Son, providing us a way out of eternal judgment and opening the door to a full relationship with Him which will last forever. Concentrating on the spiritual, it is set apart from what the world has to offer.

God's love is not emotion, but action, and He requires that our love for Him be expressed by action through obedience to His commands. As John said, when we're not willing to follow Jesus and live the life He has shown, then we're disobeying God. We are showing no love for Him, and we will not remain in His love.

When we ignore the truth of God's love, we make a conscious decision to redefine it. By changing what He intended, we even alter our concept of God. Instead of the Lord Almighty described in the Bible, this version of God is subject to what we feel He should be. In so doing, we create a more culturally acceptable god, one not so overbearing or demanding, one more tolerant of the beliefs of others, and one who, regardless of how some may ignore or even ridicule Him, still blindly loves us all, not caring whether or not we really love Him.

This is not God! It is nothing more than an idol we have made with our own hands.

❧

III

The Truth
Who Are We?

We are the temple of the living God.

2 Corinthians 6:16b

SIX

The Christian Identity

"I will say to those called 'Not my people,' 'You are my people';
and they will say, 'You are my God.'"

Hosea 2:23b

"You are my God." What a declaration! But do we really understand what these words mean?

For this statement to be true, there must be a meaningful relationship between us and God. Just as we need to understand who God is, it is also important to know who we are in relation to Him. If we fail to understand this relationship, our view of reality is distorted. We adopt beliefs not in keeping with who we really are.

Understanding the phrase *in relation to* is the key here. I am over six feet tall, enjoy backpacking, and can't stand the sight of liver, but that doesn't tell you who I am in relation to another person. To some people, I am their attorney or counselor. To others, I am their employer or friend. Who I am to them depends on the relationship we have. This relationship, in turn, is influenced by everything about us, sometimes even by our desire for control.

An important member of my family is our one-year-old West Highland Terrier, Maggie. Like a puppy, she will playfully bark and jump on toys, shoes, and even dogs much larger than herself. In her innocent desire for mischief, she will often grab a nice, clean sock, race through the house, and refuse to let go of her prey.

She may be having fun, but she has misunderstood the situation. This is not a game. The real issue, as I struggle to get my sock back, is who will control. In all her stubbornness, she will keep hanging on, even while being raised several feet in the air by a power far greater than her own. In spite of my scolding and threats, Maggie sometimes won't admit who is really in control and doesn't obey my command to release her prize. When this happens, she isn't acknowledging who she is *in relation to* the power behind the sock.

The same thing can happen in our relationship with God. If we are not clear as to who we are in relation to Him, we can easily misunderstand any given situation and not respond as a Christian should. We may not obey God's commands but choose instead to exercise our own control. Regardless of good intentions, our relationship with God and our witness of Him will suffer.

Our relationship with God is not a simple thing to be passed over lightly. His Word encourages us to explore with Him the many sides of this wonderful relationship and come to a better understanding of that power behind what we see with our eyes. In one respect, we are to be trusting children of a heavenly Father. In another, we are called to be students eagerly learning at the hands of the one true Teacher. And through it all, we are to be obedient servants of a loving Master.

We Are Not God

In our search to discover who we are in relation to God, there is a definite beginning point: *We are not God.*

That sounds easy enough to accept. After all, there are only a few people who actually claim to be God, and we see them as a bit mentally off. But look closer. These words mean much more than simply that we are not the Creator of the universe. They go directly to the issue of control. And, as is so often the case, our actions speak louder than our words.

Every day, we are urged to take control of our destiny. Television and radio commercials, newspaper ads, and scores of self-help prophets proclaim that we can be, get, and do anything we want in life. We are led through an endless array of programs, resources, seminars, books, and gadgets designed to "empower" us so that we can solve our problems, satisfy our ambitions, and improve our lives.

Regardless of the hype or the clever marketing, whether the issue is education, jobs, marriage, fitness, or financial security, the central theme is the same: "You can do anything by yourself with your own power." Through a strong positive emphasis, we are even led to believe that this is the natural order of things, that this is how everything was meant to be.

Unfortunately, we often listen to such propaganda. We may even teach it to our children. How many times has a Christian parent told his child, "God helps those who help themselves"? But that same parent will find it difficult to locate this lesson in the Bible—it isn't there!

The real problem here is that these methods, plans, and programs lead us away from God. Instead of looking to Him for guidance and help, we replace His wisdom with our own. Deep down, we want to call the shots and be in control. By doing so, we become the god in our lives. "'You shall have no other gods before me. You shall not make for yourself an idol in the form of anything in heaven above or on the earth beneath or in the waters below'" (Exod. 20:3–4).

When we try to take authority from God and look only to ourselves, we become that idol. Our intelligence, cleverness, and skill become the objects of our worship. And while we wouldn't want to admit it, we act as though we occupy God's throne and allow Him only an occasional visit.

The issue of control may be a part of the catch phrases and self-improvement philosophies of our time, but it goes all the way back to the Garden of Eden. It forms the very basis for sin, and in spite of our good intentions to make things better, it lies at the heart of our rebellion against God. Sin and the desire for control disrupt our relationship with Him and prevent us from understanding who we are in relation to God.

One mistake we often make is in thinking that when we become a Christian, our tendency to sin and our desire for control will end. Unfortunately, they remain. We still have to deal with the natural side of our lives. Even strong Christians, in subtle ways, will occasionally return to old patterns of acting, thinking, or speaking.

The blessing is that we no longer have to be ruled by sin. When Jesus came, He changed everything and gave us a new way of looking at life. "I can do everything through [God] who gives me strength" (Phil. 4:13).

Through God! Not through our own isolated efforts, but with His strength, power, and abilities that only He can provide. The passages surrounding this verse also reveal that "everything" means all that is pleasing to God and necessary to do *His* will. It is not what we may choose in order to follow the desires of *our* hearts.

A significant part of knowing who we are is admitting that sometimes we want to ignore God and cling to our own wisdom in defining how life should be. Instead of searching His Word, we fall back on "common sense," and sometimes we still have this deep desire for control—authority God has never given us.

As we come to these revelations about our personality, character, or nature, notice what has happened. This understanding of ourselves is based on who we are *in relation to* God. If we fail to look at ourselves in relation to Him, we can never really understand who we are. Only when we stand before the Light of Truth can we see ourselves in a true light.

Jim, an attorney with a large firm, once received a message from a client asking for a legal opinion regarding a tract of land she wanted to develop. Although he seldom worked in that area of the law, Jim wanted to help the client by getting a quick response for her. So he hastily prepared a memo based on his own general knowledge and sent it to her.

Unfortunately, the opinion was incorrect. The client, relying on Jim's advice, followed the wrong directions and her plans failed. Needless to say, she was very upset. She had brought to her attorney a critical situation and received only a personal opinion. As a result, she no longer trusted him and held all attorneys in low esteem.

In this case, despite meaning well, Jim made a mistake. He didn't properly accept his responsibilities to his client. He never consulted a higher authority to determine what was correct. He failed to act the way an attorney should. The consequences of Jim's actions not only affected how another person saw him, but also how she saw a much larger group of people. To the client, he was an example of all attorneys.

The point here is that because Jim did not take the time to look at himself in relation to the law he was to represent, he miscalculated his own capabilities. In that sense, he misunderstood who he really was as an attorney and never sought the higher authority for true guidance and direction.

When we understand who we are in relation to God, our Christian identity becomes clearer. It is easier to see what we should say and how we should act. We better understand our responsibilities, and our response is a Christian one. And even more importantly, we are able to present a true example of what a Christian is supposed to be. Instead of people walking away disappointed with us and disillusioned with all of Christianity (as Jim's client did regarding the entire legal profession), we can show them the light of Christ that lives in us.

Discovering our Christian identity is an exciting adventure, and it begins with acknowledging that we are not God. We were not created *like* Him, but simply as a reflection of His image. Our task is to seek and do God's will and not our own, to praise His name and not exalt ourselves, and in so doing to glorify Him always. This is at the core of our relationship with God, who guides us even further in understanding who we are through Jesus' teachings—that we are His children, students, and servants.

Children of the Father

Jesus once met a man named Nicodemus who didn't understand his relationship to God. Jesus explained, "'I tell you the truth, no one can see the kingdom of God unless he is born again. . . . no one can enter the kingdom of God unless he is born of water and the Spirit. Flesh gives birth to flesh, but the Spirit gives birth to spirit'" (John 3:3, 5–6). To help us understand who we are in relation to God, His Word refers to our transformation from nonbeliever to believer in a unique way: *rebirth*.

Just as in natural birth, this spiritual birth brings a newness, a completely new being that never before existed. As a natural birth marks the beginning of human life, so does spiritual birth announce the beginning of a person's Christian life. Therefore, in our relation to God, we first stand before Him as new creatures, "if anyone is in Christ, he is a new creation; the old has gone, the new has come!" (2 Cor. 5:17).

A newborn infant is weak and helpless. If he doesn't get care and attention, he will die. The new Christian is no different. Everything is new to him. Like a newborn baby, he must be fed spiritually if he is to grow and be an effective part of the family of God. In this second birth, he takes on a new position, a new status, and a new identity. He is no longer just another member of the human race, punching out his time in the daily grind. He has become a *child of God*.

When asked who is the greatest in the kingdom of heaven, Jesus gave a surprising answer: "'I tell you the truth, unless you change and become like little children, you will never enter the kingdom of heaven'" (Matt. 18:3). His message is clear. "Don't worry about such things in the Father's house. Don't be concerned about position or status when you get there. Be concerned about getting there!"

And how is this accomplished? We must become like children in certain very important ways. If we fail, we will never experience the love and fellowship of God.

Children Are Chosen

No child ever comes into this world simply because he decides it is time. He can't determine the day or who his parents will be. The birth of a child requires the efforts of people he doesn't know and over whom he has no control.

When a person becomes a Christian, the decision is not the product of analytical reasoning or a sense of what appears right in the world. He doesn't wake up one day and say, "After studying all the religions of the world, I like Christianity the best." He can't make himself a Christian. We have the right to become the children of God *only* because of God's action in our lives, not through anything we've done or are capable of doing. "No one can come to me unless the Father who sent me draws him, . . . no one can come to me unless the Father has enabled him'" (John 6:44, 65).

God's love and mercy must come to us before we have the slightest idea of what is going on. If God hasn't first moved in our lives, then what we may claim is a conversion experience is nothing more than an induction exercise. We haven't become children of God. We have only become members of a church.

So first we must realize that in being children of God, we are chosen.

Children Are Humble

Like a baby, the newborn Christian knows and can do very little. Of course, we are not referring to human knowledge or abilities. These relate only to our human or natural side. Here we speak in terms of the spirit.

Just as there is a lot a child learns as he grows older, there is much a Christian must learn to grow spiritually. Far too often, we rest on our accomplishments and feel intelligent and wise. But as the prophets often said, the intelligence and wisdom of man are utter foolishness compared to the wisdom of God.

A Christian has to learn and relearn, studying God's Word for truth. He must be willing to say that his genius and talents count for nothing except as God may decide to use them. He must humble himself and realize that, just as a human baby, he is helpless and completely dependent on God. "'"They will all be taught by God." Everyone who listens to the Father and learns from him comes to me'" (John 6:45). "'Whoever humbles himself like this child is the greatest in the kingdom of heaven'" (Matt. 18:4).

Children Have Acceptance and Faith

I have three wonderful children, and though each is a different person, they all share one thing in common. They trust me. When they were small, I could throw them in the air, catch them, spin them around, and they would never even blink an eye. Oh, sometimes it would bother their mother, but they were having fun. Fearless? No. They just trusted me and had faith that I wouldn't drop them.

All of us begin life this way. We have a blind faith and trust in those around us. As we get older, the faith and trust slowly disappear. We experience the falls, the hurt, the emotions, the disappointment, and sometimes the betrayal. We put up walls, allowing only those who prove their worthiness to come into our lives. To all others, the door is closed.

When a person becomes a Christian, the hardest barriers to overcome are the walls he has erected in his life. Though they may have protected him from pain and suffering, they also effectively inhibit his relationship with God. Jesus again tells us to look to the children. "People were bringing little children to Jesus to have him touch them, but the disciples rebuked them. When Jesus saw this, he was indignant. He said to them, 'Let the little children come to me, and do not hinder them, for the kingdom of God belongs to such as these. I tell you the truth, anyone who will not receive the kingdom of God like a little child will never enter it'" (Mark 10:13–15).

Children are open and spontaneous in the way they express their acceptance and faith. While others had brought them to Jesus, the children had no hesitancy in going to Him, being wrapped in His arms, and receiving His blessing. They accepted His love and His gift without question or doubt. There were no barriers.

Jesus tells us that if we are to be children of God, we should do the same and be willing openly and immediately to accept His love and gift of eternal salvation. We can't hesitate or put things off until some time that better suits us. And He wants us, without any question or doubt, to accept Him for who He is—not caring what others may think or where we may be. God wants our complete acceptance.

He also desires our sincere faith, and in a special way. Our faith in God cannot rest on what we have seen, felt, or experienced. Instead, it must have a foundation that is totally opposite from what we normally require. "Now faith is being sure of what we hope for and certain of what we do not see" (Heb. 11:1).

God could not have chosen a way to define our faith that is more in conflict with human nature and human teachings. Most of our knowledge is gained through learning by example or by doing. We have *faith* in ourselves because we have learned how to do something.

For example, I have faith that I can drive my car to work. Why? Because I have learned how to drive and which roads to take. Even if I get lost, I've learned how to read a map (though maybe not how to ask for directions).

But this kind of *faith* is not what God is talking about. Our concept of faith relies on personal knowledge or logical conclusions based on our learning and experience. We are raised to believe that everything must be felt, seen, heard, smelled, tried, analyzed, and proven to verify its existence. This faith depends on *us* providing our own assurance.

Faith in God does not rely on knowledge, logic, conclusions, learning, or experience. It bears no relation to our IQ or our ability to conduct scientific experiments. This kind of faith depends on *God* providing His assurance.

While understanding faith is essential, it is also important to realize the message that a lack of faith sends to the world. "And without faith it is impossible to please God, because anyone who comes to him must believe that he exists and that he rewards those who earnestly seek him" (Heb. 11:6).

If we don't have faith in God, if we don't believe the promises He has given us, and if we fail to put our trust in Him and live as He has taught, it's as though we were shouting to the world: "God does not exist!"

We tell the world that our God is a God of judgment and mercy who loves all and wants all to be with Him forever. We claim the only way to this life is through Christ Jesus and through obeying His commands in how we should live. But our actions tell a different story. We don't love or care for each other in a selfless way, putting the needs of others ahead of our own. We allow people to walk the streets, living without shelter, clothing, and decent food. We don't provide medical attention to all of the sick and dying. We hoard our money and think only of ourselves. Worst of all, we choose not to take advantage of countless opportunities to tell others of Jesus, His sacrifice for us, and the eternal life that God can provide.

The world hears our idle chatter but sees reality in our actions. How can it know that we believe what the Bible says? For if we did, given the joy of eternal life on the one hand and the horror of eternal torment on the other, wouldn't we obey Christ's commands? When we don't, the world reaches the logical conclusion that Bible stories are mere fantasy and that God is just a part of our imagination.

Faith is at the center of a Christian's life. Without it, he or she cannot be a child of God. When we come to terms with what true faith really is, we are on the road to knowing God more intimately and doing His will more effectively.

Children Are Loved

Many people share a common problem: a deep loss of self-worth rooted in the belief that they are not loved. The need to be loved and to know we are loved is tremendously important. When that need is not met, depression, anxiety, and frustration take hold.

Children especially need this assurance. They don't have the benefit of the knowledge and experience of adults. They can't sit back and say things will get better. They have no way of knowing; they have nothing to use for comparison.

In the average home, parents naturally know that small children need a lot of affection. They shower them with hugs and kisses, and the children often cuddle up next to Mom or Dad. When Jesus said to become like children, He was also referring to this love relationship that exists between parent and child. Our heavenly Father loves and cares for us as His children in the same way a loving parent would for a son or daughter.

To emphasize this point, Jesus demonstrated His love for the children, taking them in His arms and blessing them. Those children knew Jesus cared. "How great is the love the Father has lavished on us, that we should be called children of God! And that is what we are!" (1 John 3:1a).

John tells us that even though we were separated from God and condemned to die because of our sin, we can be reconciled and experience His fellowship. In one of his letters, John stresses that God's love does not depend on our love for Him. "We love because he first loved us" (1 John 4:19).

God doesn't respond to us because we have shown some affection for Him. He loved us even *before* we loved Him. As we grow spiritually and learn how to love Him, we have the assurance that even with the full knowledge of who we are and what we would do, God loved us first and cares for us deeply.

Children Praise God

There's one part of Christian life which seldom receives the attention it deserves: praising God. "When the chief priests and the teachers of the law saw the wonderful things he did and the children shouting in the temple area, 'Hosanna to the Son of David,' they were indignant. 'Do you hear what these children are saying?' they asked him. 'Yes,' replied Jesus, 'have you never read, "From the lips of children and infants you have ordained praise"?'" (Matt. 21:15–16).

In this passage, the word *ordained* is used to project the idea that God has set aside and prescribed praise from His children. Jesus was quoting Psalm 8:2, which specifically uses the Hebrew word for *ordained*. Other translations use the literal Greek word which means "perfected," showing that perfect praise comes from children. God wants us to understand that both are at work.

Praise is required of all of us and should be taken seriously. Peter clearly tells us that being a Christian involves praising God. "But you are a chosen people, a royal priesthood, a holy nation, a people belonging to God, that you may declare the praises of him who called you out of darkness into his wonderful light" (1 Pet. 2:9).

But if praise is so important, why do we hear so little about it today? Maybe we don't understand what praise really is.

Praise is not sitting in a service, listening to a sermon, or hearing the beautiful words of a hymn. It isn't merely teaching a Bible class or cleaning up the church lawn. And we don't find it simply in the administration of the congregation's affairs. All of these are significant activities, but *alone* they are not praise.

We make a mistake when we define praise in terms of what is seen on the outside. An emotional display or devotion to a particular church activity doesn't always tell what lies in a person's heart. Sometimes what we call a time of praise is simply people going through the motions of a religious routine. A better definition, combining the concepts of worship, reverence, and esteem, would be the following: Praise is an act, process, or instance through which great respect, honor, and devotion are shown toward something highly regarded, valued, and prized. Praise then is an outward expression of something deeply held, felt, and believed. It is not a ritualistic action, but a demonstrated attitude.

If we praise God through song, it is because we believe the words and proclaim the message they bear of Him. The flow of instruments, the beautiful harmony, and the talent of a choir provide an avenue for worship, but they are not praise in and of themselves. If the music is not an expression of a singer's personal respect, honor, and devotion to God, whom that person highly regards, values, and prizes, then the finest singing in all the world will never rise above the level of idle chatter in the ears of our heavenly Father.

And while singing is an easy example, this understanding of praise applies to everything we do, whether or not we happen to be in a church sanctuary. If we teach, we should do it in a manner that praises God. If we listen to a sermon, lead a youth group, or clean the church building, we should be doing it so as to praise God. At work, in the grocery store, at the dinner table, or on vacation, we can offer praise to our Lord.

True praise begins in the heart where it grows as an expression of our relationship with God. It is not a fleeting or changing emotion nor an expression of human sentimentality. We don't praise Him out of some warm and fuzzy feeling.

Praise is an attitude and a part of the foundation for who we are in relation to God. We praise Him because we are His children.

We Are Children

As I have grown older and the world has become a more complicated place, I occasionally have found myself thinking how nice it would be to return to a childhood when times were innocent and life simpler. It would be wonderful to be a child again with no responsibilities or cares, never having to answer to anyone or meet someone else's deadlines.

Yet if we are being honest, our childhood was never really like that. It was a time of growth and change, and even as children, sometimes things didn't always go the way we planned. There was plenty of anxiety, frustration, and pain along with all the fun, happiness, and joy. It was a time of learning—learning what was important, how to care, and how to be responsible.

Sometimes when we speak of becoming children of God, we have that same wishful dreamland in mind. We want our Christian life to be only a time of happiness and laughter, without problems or concerns. However, just as it wasn't true in our natural childhood, it isn't the reality of our Christian life either. This, too, is a time of learning.

As children of God, we cast aside an old way of life to learn a new one. In this spiritual education, we find that we are individually chosen by God, who dearly loves us, to become a part of His family. We learn how to become dependent on Him; express our faith in a way that is open, immediate, and complete; and praise Him. And, when it comes to letting others see Christ in our lives, we learn that we have a responsibility for which we are ultimately accountable to Him.

Above all, we begin to discover our Christian identity: who we are in relation to God. As we learn and grow, our relationship with Him becomes stronger and He gives us, as gifts to His children, a deeper peace and more satisfying joy than we have ever known.

This is something really special. After all, we are not just anybody's kids; we are children of the Father!

c∞ɔ

Students of the Teacher

As soon as a child is born, the process of learning begins. As an infant, he learns how to crawl, walk, and speak. He learns about objects, shapes, and colors. Then he enters formal education, spending the next twelve years studying everything from how to read and write to chemistry and physics. This may even continue several more years if he pursues a bachelor's, master's, or doctoral degree.

Though school will eventually end, learning never does. When we enter the ranks of the employed, we have to learn how to do our job. After the car has broken down for the last time, we learn how to get a loan. And when we have finally bought our first house, we learn how to take care of the lawn, fix sinks, wire a ceiling fan, and what every "do-it-your-selfer" needs to know—how to put out an electrical fire.

We grow older each day, but we can't stop learning if we're going to keep up in this ever-changing world. The same is true for us as Christians.

When we accept Christ as our Lord and Savior, we have a lot to learn if we are to grow in God's knowledge, understanding, and wisdom. Unfortunately, many equate human knowledge with spiritual maturity and never see the importance of a serious spiritual education. Yet without such study and learning, we can no more understand all it means to be a Christian than a three-year-old can know how to fly a plane. And if we don't grow in that understanding, we can't grow in our relationship with God.

We are not only children, we are also students.

Respect the Textbook

Once we put our egos aside and admit that there is quite a bit to learn, the next step in our education is to accept the textbook. For Christians this should be simple, since we claim to believe that the Bible is the Word of God. But even though it has long been a source of education, we have allowed it to be banned in most of our country's schools.

How should Christians view this book? In his charge to Timothy, Paul stressed the importance of God's Word: "From infancy you have known the holy Scriptures, which are able to make you wise for salvation through faith in Christ Jesus. All Scripture is God-breathed and is useful for teaching, rebuking, correcting and training in righteousness, so that the man of God may be thoroughly equipped for every good work" (2 Tim. 3:15–17).

It was critical to Paul that Timothy study the Scriptures. What he would gain was simply too important to miss.

And what was this important prize? Paul points out that the Scriptures are God-breathed; in other words, they exist through the inspiration of God. These aren't simply the words of men. God Himself has had His holy hand in the writing and preservation of these documents.

The Scriptures also provide us with the knowledge and understanding of our salvation in Christ Jesus. When we hear a sermon, its influence on our lives is through the authority of the Bible. Without a Biblical foundation, it is nothing more than the opinion of an individual in a lonely pulpit. But when rooted in the Word of God, the message has power. We know we are hearing God's commands and not one person's desires.

Also notice that Paul specifically mentions the *continuing* worth of the Scriptures, calling them useful for teaching, rebuking, correcting, and training in righteousness. Take careful note as to whom all of this is directed. Is there a restriction? Does Paul say the Bible is useful only for teaching others?

No! The Bible continues as a resource of instruction for *us*. We never learn it all. We will always be learning, seeking to understand more as we draw closer to God.

Finally, Paul points out that our continuing study of the Scriptures is necessary for us to be thoroughly equipped for any good work God may choose. Obviously this doesn't happen in a few minutes or in the course of a single Bible study. Our spiritual education continues throughout our lives.

In accepting the Bible as our textbook, we also must understand its power and approach our study seriously. "The word of God is living and active. Sharper than any double-edged sword, it penetrates even to dividing soul and spirit, joints and marrow; it judges the thoughts and attitudes of the heart" (Heb. 4:12).

Living and active. The Bible is not a history book or a collection of old stories. God's Word is alive today! Though written centuries ago, it applies to every aspect of our lives now, holding the standards for how we should live and relate to one another. The Bible continues as the written authority for the Christian life.

In spite of this, I'm afraid many Christians have forgotten the importance of the Bible and regard it as just another reference book. They quickly turn to other sources for their answers instead of first looking to God's Word.

We need to recognize the significance of the Bible in our lives, study it continuously, and teach it to our children. If our lives are not founded on the Word of God, our faith will become a shallow reflection of what God wants it to be. The Bible must be our number-one textbook for living, with everything else relegated to second place.

Respect the Teacher

In schools across the nation, there is a serious threat to our educational system—a severe lack of respect for teachers. Every day, men and women face classrooms overflowing with children who are unruly, defiant, and sometimes violent. These students fail to learn because they have no respect for the teacher, and without that respect, they won't even listen.

Christians are students in a great spiritual classroom. We have the unique opportunity to gain understanding, wisdom, and knowledge greater than anything we can possibly imagine. So why aren't churches overflowing with eager and excited believers who want to grow and learn?

The answer is very simple: We don't respect the Teacher or give Him the honor He is due! Now before you scream "Blasphemy!" and start hunting for firewood to burn the heathen lawyer, carefully consider the following.

Jesus made a crucial observation about this teacher-student relationship, saying, "'Nor are you to be called "teacher," for you have one Teacher, the Christ'" (Matt. 23:10). Here Jesus tells us three things about a teacher of the faith: (1) There has been only one in the past; (2) there is only one now; and (3) there will be only one in the future.

That one is Jesus. He bluntly says, "There's only one teacher and I'm it." Period. No discussion. But why was this so important that Jesus had to tell His followers? The answer lies in our human nature which He understood only too well.

Remember today's out-of-control classrooms? These kids have no respect for their teachers because they're convinced that they already know what they need to survive. Everything else is useless. When they see no value in what a teacher can offer, they effectively remove his status as teacher. He can no longer teach because, at the very least, they consider themselves his equals.

Many of us act the same way toward God. Because of a natural desire for independence and control, we don't go to Him or study His Word—as if we know enough to solve our problems or at least to get by. We fail to respect Him for *His* knowledge, wisdom, and guidance. *Respect* is the key here.

Jesus distinguished His Teacher-student relationship from the usual teacher-student relationship. In the latter, there will always be a termination point because there is only so much that can be taught. When a student learns everything the teacher knows, they are equals and the teaching ends.

The Teacher-student relationship we have with Jesus is different. We will never learn all He knows or be equal with Him. This Teacher-student relationship and our education will last forever. Just as we are always children, we are also always students, learning continually at the hand of the risen Lord.

And our goal? To strive to be trained fully so that we can be *like* Jesus. We study at the hand of our Teacher so that we can better understand what it means to be a Christian. We learn so that others can see Christ in our actions, in our words, and in our lives. When we do this, we bring glory and honor to our Lord, for we have become true witnesses of Him to a lost world.

⚬∞⚬

NINE

Servants of the Master

When Jesus explained what it means to be a disciple, He often referred to His followers as children and students. We are comfortable with such gentle images. They make us feel wanted as God's beloved children and privileged as His special students. But there is another analogy Jesus used that is equally significant, though sometimes less welcome and often ignored—that of a servant.

Somehow we have the idea that as soon as a person becomes a Christian, his or her entire way of acting and thinking immediately changes. The new Christian suddenly begins to care for the sick, support widows and orphans, and generally pursue the life of Christ with a never-ending enthusiasm. But this seldom occurs.

Certainly people go through life-changing experiences. After all, that is what conversion is all about. There is a hunger to know more about Jesus and be on that mountaintop with God.

Unfortunately, the mountaintop experience doesn't last. There will be lows as well as highs. God never promised us a rose garden, and if we are living as Christians in this world which the prince of darkness calls home, we'll find plenty of thorns.

But even when times are rough or we feel drawn back to our old way of life, Jesus still calls us to follow Him. If I may borrow from an advertising campaign, sometimes being a Christian simply requires that we "just do it!" No questioning the wisdom behind a command. No searching for an explanation. And especially no waiting until we feel like doing it. At this stage in our growth, it's not so important to dwell on some feeling we may or may not have as it is to *just do it.* If God said it, that settles it. Now do it.

Jesus called this *obeying.*

The Master-Servant Relationship

In his letter to the Philippians, Paul carefully described the attitude Christians should have: "Your attitude should be the same as that of Christ Jesus: Who, being in very nature God, did not consider equality with God something to be grasped, but made himself nothing, taking the very nature of a servant, being made in human likeness. And being found in appearance as a man, he humbled himself and became obedient to death—even death on a cross!" (Phil. 2:5–8).

Child—student—and now servant. Isn't this interesting? Normally we have to prove ourselves worthy during a trial period before we are admitted into any organization or group. But God reverses the order! He *begins* by fully accepting us into His wonderful family. Through His love, we progress in our Christian growth from child to student to servant.

As servants, we are called to humble ourselves and obey, following the example Jesus set. Yet we are not to be servants to other people. Instead, we are to serve God. Christ alone is our Master. No one else.

Far too often we misunderstand servanthood, seeing it simply as good deeds which we do for others. We become involved in charities, efforts to cure diseases, and programs for the less fortunate. Then we sit back, fold our arms, and say, "It is good."

But we have missed something important here. While such efforts are needed, they all have a single common goal: happiness in *this* life. And the means to this end is through serving *people.*

Jesus certainly wants us to help others, but that is only part of what He expects. Our goal is also happiness, but with a view toward *eternal* life. And we achieve it by serving *God.*

During His last meal with the disciples, Jesus did something that disturbed them so much that Peter at first refused to participate. Jesus performed the menial task of a slave and washed their feet.

"'Do you understand what I have done for you? . . . You call me "Teacher" and "Lord," and rightly so, for that is what I am. Now that I, your Lord and Teacher, have washed your feet, you also should wash one another's feet. I have set you an example that you should do as I have done for you. I tell you the truth, no servant is greater than his master, nor is a messenger greater than the one who sent him. Now that you know these things, you will be blessed if you do them'" (John 13:12b–17).

By this act, Jesus did much more than tell His followers to humble themselves and take care of their fellow man. He struck at the very heart of their relationship with God.

Notice that when Jesus referred to the titles His disciples had given Him, He said *Teacher* and *Lord*. But when He claimed these titles and acknowledged who He was before them, He reversed the order to *Lord* and then *Teacher*. This was not a play on words. The task He had performed emphasized His point to the disciples. What Jesus was saying was simply this: "Yes. You're correct in saying that I am your Teacher, but more importantly, I am your Lord. I am your Master, and you are My servant. You do not serve mankind, you serve Me. Just as no servant is ever above his master, you are not above Me. You will always be My servant, and you will always have the obligation of obeying Me."

Jesus wasn't teaching about social responsibility. He wasn't calling us to a life of building shelters, working in food kitchens, or protecting the environment. *These are secondary!*

Christians, to be Christlike, must be servants who acknowledge God as their Master and follow the example of Christ, who became the ultimate servant. If we cannot rise above our Lord who is Christ Jesus and if our Lord was the servant of God, then how can we be masters of our own destiny or rulers of our own fate?

"'No servant can serve two masters. Either he will hate the one and love the other, or he will be devoted to the one and despise the other'" (Luke 16:13a).

God is the *only* master Christians are to serve.

The Obedience Factor

One of the most often used phrases among Christians is "Jesus is Lord." We hear it in the sanctuary and sing it in our hymns. We even place it on cute banners and bumper stickers. But do we understand what it means?

The essence of the Master-servant relationship is rooted in obedience. Usually this word is softened by substituting the word *serving*. Because of pride and ego, we prefer to say that we are *serving* our Lord. It has a pious ring to it and sounds more like a nice gesture on our part.

But to be honest, Jesus didn't say He wanted us to *serve* Him, but to *obey* Him. Though they appear the same, the difference is significant in defining our relationship with God. We obey because we are told to, not necessarily because of any personal desire to do so. Sometimes the only desire that exists is to obey the will of God, and we do so even though we would much rather be doing something else.

Parents often have to remind a child to brush his teeth, use soap when he takes a bath, come in out of the rain, and, worst of all, do homework. Many children don't want to do these things, but they do anyway because they are obeying their parents, not because they are serving them.

God never said being a Christian would be easy, but He does tell us how we should live. Unfortunately, we often want to do something completely different from what He wants. But if we really are the servants of God, living by Christ's example, we know that our personal desires have nothing to do with the situation. It is only necessary that we obey.

This is not to say that our attitude isn't important. However, even when it is not the best in the world, we still must obey. We don't have the right to wait until our frame of mind is better. Oddly enough, sometimes a correct mental attitude actually follows the act.

A few years ago I was invited to attend a social function, and I knew a certain person would be there. We had once engaged in a very heated argument, and I still bore some ill feelings. Although I had frequently taught about Christ's command to reconcile, I had failed to do so in this case. In fact, I really didn't want to. With this attitude in hand, I decided not to attend. Thankfully, the Holy Spirit would not leave me alone with my decision, and I ultimately obeyed.

There are two points worth noting here. First, I did not *want* to follow Jesus' command to try and reconcile. I still had some bad feelings and wanted to wait until the time was better, like maybe a hundred years later. Even when I did go, the experience was difficult. But the bottom line was that I went. I obeyed my Master's command.

Second, everything eventually worked out fine, not because we became fast friends, but because God took away my anger, the bitter root that was still affecting my life. Remember Jesus' promise? "'Now that you know these things, you will be blessed if you do them'" (John 13:17). God blessed me in this very real and unexpected way.

Because we are human, we remain vulnerable to our natural side with its potential for anger, hatred, jealousy, and spite. Yet we're called to live by seeking and doing God's will. There will be times when our emotions and desires get in the way and even become greater than our ability to handle them. At those times, we have to turn them over to God and admit that, by our own power, we can't change the way we feel. Because we are Christians and servants of the risen Lord, we still carry on and obey God, regardless of how we feel. He will take our emotions and desires and change them according to His will.

Obedience Is Love

Because we are often driven by personal desires, Jesus used obedience to define our love for Him. "'Whoever has my commands and obeys them, he is the one who loves me'" (John 14:21a).

Four times during the Last Supper, Jesus spoke of what it means to really love Him. Real love is not an emotion. It's not made up of personal desires, wants, or needs. Love for Christ is found in one thing only—our obedience to Him. If we truly love Jesus, we will obey His commands. Pure and simple.

The reverse is also true. If we refuse to follow Jesus, we do not love Him. We may go to church, sing hymns, or teach a Bible class; but if we don't obey His commands and follow His teachings, laying all else aside and living the life He has ordained, we do not love Jesus. When we tell others we love Him, *we are liars and frauds, and our witness counts for nothing!*

Jesus must be our Lord if He is to be our Savior. There must be the Master-servant relationship in which we are willing to obey His commands. Otherwise, we play a game and try to call it *Christianity*.

But the true Christian does love Jesus and seek to follow His will, even when his emotions and desires may try to draw him away. He is a servant of the risen Lord.

The Growing Christian

Understanding who we are in relation to God is not an easy task. The process continues throughout our lives as God gives us new opportunities to learn and grow. Only the basics have been presented here. The fine tuning, the deeper lessons, and the one-on-one instruction must come from God Himself.

We are all different in our Christian growth and our ability to understand, so God treats each of us differently. What one may see immediately, another may take a lifetime to find.

It is important that we welcome God's efforts to grow us into the people He wants. We are His children, and He has much for us to share. We are His students, and He has much for us to learn. We are His servants, and He has much for us to do.

As we follow and draw closer to God, He draws closer to us. He keeps His promises and we gain wisdom, knowledge, and understanding. Our love for Him grows, and our fellowship with Him becomes intimate.

It was this special, close relationship to which Christ referred when He told the disciples, "'You are my friends if you do what I command. I no longer call you servants, because a servant does not know his master's business. Instead, I have called you friends, for everything that I have learned from my Father I have made known to you'" (John 15:14–15). Christians, those people who sincerely strive to be like Christ, are His friends and share an intimate relationship with the heavenly Father. We are no longer a part of this world, just as Christ is not a part of this world. We simply have a mission here—to do the will of God and, by so doing, be His example for those who don't know Him. As we grow closer to God, we fulfill His instruction that we become more like Christ, thereby becoming more holy.

By understanding who we are in relation to God, we begin to see the importance of our witness to the world and our personal involvement in getting the true message to people everywhere. We have the advantage because we know the truth. But we must allow that truth to shine through us to a lost world.

We are God's people, His students, and His servants. We are loved, chosen, taught, trained, disciplined, and encouraged. We grow spiritually each day in order to do better the work that He alone determines. And we tell the world that He is God, whose Son sacrificed Himself in our place so that we might be reconciled with the Father and have the promise of eternal life. We bear this good news in the prayer that others may also be drawn by the Holy Spirit to come to God through Jesus Christ and know, like us, that in His eyes they too are special. "You are a chosen people, a royal priesthood, a holy nation, a people belonging to God, that you may declare the praises of him who called you out of darkness into his wonderful light" (1 Pet. 2:9).

IV

The Witness
In the Home

The LORD's curse is on the house of the wicked,
but he blesses the home of the righteous.

Proverbs 3:33

⸎

Lost without a Home

The façade of Christianity begins within a person's heart, slowly influencing attitudes and actions until it becomes a natural part of life. Its most meaningful growth is in the home, that place of security where we can relax and be ourselves. Here we can be seen for who we really are, without the exterior often worn for friends and neighbors.

Those who hide behind a façade of Christianity are a key factor in the destruction of the family. A vibrant family involves the interaction of husband and wife, parent and child. But sometimes these interactions create so much disruption that marriages, childhoods, and relationships are ruined. Far too often, the injury is deep and the scar, permanent.

Irretrievably Broken

Divorces are tragic, horrible events. For many, they resolve nothing, acting only as an intermission until a new marriage raises the curtain for old actors to resume their roles. The inner problems remain.

When people seek a divorce, sometimes they can be guided through their difficulties and helped to reestablish the relationship they thought was lost forever. Unfortunately, most have closed minds. They have decided it's time for a change and refuse to turn back. Revenge may even become involved. The yelling, bickering, hurting, and destruction continue.

Many of these cases involve marriages in which both the husband and wife claim to be Christians. Throughout my years of counseling, however, I've noticed a curious fact. In every case, the actual cause of the divorce was simply a failure to be Christian.

The reasons given for why a divorce is *needed* are long and varied, from selfishness and apathy to illicit affairs and spousal abuse. Yet I have never heard anyone say, "He doesn't act like a Christian anymore." This just isn't bad enough. They have to strike deeper.

But there's probably another reason. If they do mention the *un-christian* ways of the other, it will probably be thrown back in their face. They may even have to admit that they could be part of the problem. Even worse, their Christianity might also remind them of something called *forgiveness*.

In most cases there are problems on both sides. I have yet to see a divorce in which some fault was not shared. At times there is a real need for psychological counseling or involvement by the proper authorities, but that's not the norm. The average divorce simply involves people "who have fallen out of love." As the law coldly puts it, the marriage is irretrievably broken. No specifics. No knives thrown or guns fired. The marriage is just over.

So how is this affected by a casual Christian? How does he intensify the problem, encouraging the destruction of the family?

First, remember that he merely plays at being a Christian. He hasn't accepted the responsibilities that go with the Christian life. Most of all, he doesn't understand the true meaning of love.

Tony Campolo tells a story concerning the time when he was working on his college degree. It seems the psychology department had decided the best way for a student to learn to be a counselor was to put him in real counseling situations. It was also a cheap way for many people to get some form of counseling.

One man often came to Mr. Campolo complaining about his wife. He moaned that she no longer filled his desires and they didn't enjoy the same things. Finally one day, the man showed up for his usual appointment and announced his decision to divorce his wife. His reason was simple. He just didn't love her anymore.

Mr. Campolo turned to him and said, "I don't believe you've ever known what love is."

Those who hide behind a façade of Christianity are primarily concerned with their own satisfaction. They never look to God for guidance or to His Word for instruction. As a result, they don't understand the truth of what love really is. Jesus said: "'My command is this: Love each other as I have loved you. Greater love has no one than this, that he lay down his life for his friends'" (John 15:12–13).

Jesus taught that love involves making sacrifices, placing another person's interests ahead of our own. When we truly love someone, we want what is best for him or her, and we seek to bring it about. I have witnessed firsthand the depth of that kind of love.

True Love

In 1983, my family was jolted by some horrible news. My father was diagnosed as having amyotrophic lateral sclerosis, more commonly known as Lou Gehrig's disease. Almost always fatal, it affects the nerves that control the muscles, causing them to malfunction and wither away. Men and women—who could run and jump, play golf and tennis, and roll around on the floor with their children and grandchildren—slowly become invalids, incapable of even speaking.

Though my father was very active and only fifty years old, he was given just two years to live. However, the doctors couldn't see another factor that was powerfully present in my father's life—the depth of my mother's love.

In his remaining years, my mother was always there. As his condition became worse, she became strong. At first she just helped him button his shirts. Later, she dressed him completely. She cooked for him, fed him, and wiped his mouth. He was always clean, his hair combed, and, as much as possible, he was comfortable.

Because of true love, my father astounded the doctors and nurses who checked on him. Yes, the disease was fatal, but he lived almost seven years, not the two that had been predicted. He saw three more grandchildren born and his sons succeed in their work. Most of all, he had the rare opportunity to experience a love that was real and full and always there.

A casual Christian doesn't understand true love. Focused on *his* satisfaction, he ultimately looks for what will make *him* happy. He becomes obsessed with physical attraction, sexual relations, and how the other person makes him feel. This "love" revolves around his own wants and desires.

Whether it's a night at the theatre, evening dinners in expensive restaurants and stimulating conversation, or perhaps nights out at the ballpark, meals prepared on time, and no interruptions during a favorite TV show, this person rapidly moves from the thrill of romance to "fulfilling my needs." For such people, marriage is not the union described in the Bible, but a convenience in their lives.

When their marriage encounters the least bit of difficulty, they wonder if they've made a mistake. They were told love means never having to say you're sorry, that it holds eternal joy and happiness. And sadly, they bought into the fantasy.

The fact is, love does involve conflict. There will always be times of hurt feelings, bitterness, and frustration, but real love allows us to calm down, work through the rough times, and grow into the union the Bible proclaims. Why? Because in real love, the happiness of one is the cause of happiness for the other.

But for casual Christians, this act is just too hard to follow. Marriage isn't what they always dreamed it would be. The husband changes or the wife becomes different. The things they held in common no longer hold any importance. They say, "We've fallen out of love and it's time for a change."

The result: divorce, custody battles, child support and alimony hearings, bitterness, hatred, separation, and destruction. The man and woman are freed from each other, having learned nothing. And if there are children, they will bear the scars for the rest of their lives.

Instead of setting an example of Christ's love, the casual Christian shows just the opposite. He even tells others that Christians are not immune from divorce any more than anybody else. He shrugs his shoulders and admits that he's just like the rest of the world.

In this way, he projects an image of a Christian that is false. Instead of being Christlike, he is worldlike, just another soul in the sea of humanity. The Christ we are to represent seems just a dream, incompatible with the lives of real people who must live and work in a real world.

⤮

ELEVEN

Suffer Not the Children

While divorces disrupt the lives of adults, children become victims long before their parents venture into a courtroom. Marital conflict, though devastating to a family, is just a part of the horrible effect casual Christians can have on the lives of their children. In fact, it doesn't matter if the parents get along. The harm can flourish just fine in quiet, *loving* families. For behind the façade of Christianity is deception, and whether intentional or not, the actions of those caught in its lies produce a lesson in contradiction.

Look through the eyes of children. What they believe to be true in this world is formed by what they see, hear, and experience. The first impact is found in the home, made by the people who have the responsibility of raising them.

On Sunday morning, casual Christians take their children to church where they hear of God's love, how we should treat one another, and how important it is to spread the gospel. These children may even see their parents sing in the choir or give the congregational prayer.

Then on the way home, reality sets in. They watch as their father cuts in front of others on the highway or passes someone with a flat tire. They see their parents walk quickly past a man shivering in the night as they hurry into a restaurant. They join their parents in watching one TV show after another filled with murders, rapes, lies, and immorality. And what do they receive from their parents? No comment, instruction, or disapproval. Just silent acceptance.

Television alone can easily distort the truth for children. On many shows, Christianity is portrayed as a fellowship of fools and hypocrites. We often see a minister or church member presented as an arrogant, biased, and self-righteous prude, secretly violating the rules he seeks to impose on others. Is this the truth?

Television also consistently degrades Christianity while promoting mystical religions and far-out beliefs. I recently saw a comedy that included a scene in which a young man was involved in calling a spirit guide to help him. Are these the lessons we want children to learn?

The issue here is not the quality of television or the amount of time children sit mesmerized in front of the set, though both should be important concerns for every family. The ultimate problem is the silence of Christian parents. Children sit for hours watching, listening, and learning. Yet seldom do we point out that the behavior they see, the words they hear, or the beliefs the actors claim are wrong. Through such silence, television becomes the instructor in their search for truth.

A façade of Christianity provides the perfect setting for this to occur. The casual Christian has never learned the tremendous importance that God's Word places on the education that should come from parents or the incredible responsibility they have in providing it. He has ignored, or probably never heard, the Bible's plea to the child: "Hold on to instruction, do not let it go; guard it well, for it is your life" (Prov. 4:13).

Instead, he seeks to protect himself and tries to shift the blame. "After all," he says, "I'm not the one who said those things." He even reasons, "Everyone knows you can't believe what you see on TV."

And so, when it suits his purpose, he attributes to children abilities of discernment that come only with experience and maturity. Later, when the unexpected occurs, he finds himself wondering how they could have done such things, thought such ideas, or uttered such words.

He also has a ready argument, usually one involving work, for not spending time with his children. How often have we heard: "I'd really like to spend more time with my kids, but I have too much work to do right now. I'll make it up to them later," or "My work is important, and there are so many people depending on me. I'm sure they understand," or "I have to work long hours just to keep food on the table and a roof over our heads. There's no more time left in the day. That's just the way it is."

Sometimes these are indeed noble, important, and even self-sacrificing reasons. They apply to many different people, from the corporate executive to the housewife, from the minister to the auto worker. They even apply to lawyers.

But for the casual Christian, these seemingly righteous explanations are nothing more than poor excuses. They reflect a consistent pattern of conduct rather than the exception to the rule. The bottom line is that he has chosen to withdraw from his children, leaving their education, maturity, and future in the hands of others. He never seems to understand what he is required to do—*regardless of his work!*

Those involved in ministry work have to be especially careful here. This applies whether the person is a pastor, minister, elder, deacon, Bible study leader, assistant, encourager, or one of many workers. Each has been led by God to a particular calling, one deemed to be very important in carrying out God's work in this world, and rightly so.

But sometimes one specific ministry can be given such priority that other responsibilities which also require attention are ignored, abandoned, or simply left to others. Under the right circumstances, the special ministry may develop an *exclusive* nature that God never intended. When that happens, well-meaning people thoughtlessly become devoted to the calling itself rather than to the One who did the calling.

I once attended a conference in which one of the speakers was a prominent, retired preacher. During his portion of the program, he related a personal experience to demonstrate the level of commitment he felt Christians needed when it came to work within the church.

All my life I've been completely devoted to God and His work. I've preached several times every Sunday, led week-long revivals, filled in for sick pastors, spoken at Christian conferences, taught Bible studies, traveled on foreign missions, and taken advantage of every opportunity to preach and teach. Any time anyone ever asked me to do something, I was there. I've never let anything stand in the way, even when it was something I personally wanted real bad.

I remember one time when my son came up to me. I'd been away for several weeks, preaching at other churches as I was accustomed to doing, and I was packing my bags to leave again for another three weeks. My boy looked up at me with tears running down his cheeks and said, "Daddy, please don't go. Please stay home with me."

Even though it hurt, I told my son that I had to go and do God's work, and then I sent him back to his mother. In fact, she really raised all of our children by herself. I wasn't around very much while they were growing up. I didn't help them with their homework or play catch in the front yard. And most of the time, I couldn't be there for birthdays or when they received awards at school. But you see, you have to be committed if you're going to do God's work.

Unfortunately for his children, this preacher forgot that "doing God's work" also involves the education, training, and raising of his children as Christians. This is a very important part of the calling of any Christian parent. And nowhere in the Bible does God remove that responsibility.

This is not a condemnation of those who have rough times in their work, whatever that may be. All parents have times when they can't be with their children as they would like. However, it is a warning to those who put themselves and their work ahead of the welfare of their children. It is a declaration: *God has commanded that the raising and instruction of our children as Christians is to hold a place of utmost importance in our lives.*

Remember the hidden motivation of the casual Christian? He seeks his own satisfaction, and his work becomes a significant part of how he defines his self-worth. Take away the work and you take away his self-esteem.

This hidden motivation is found in all walks of life, not just in the corporate world where we expect a cutthroat "rise to the top as fast as you can" existence. It's also in the housewife for whom managing the house becomes an obsession. There are rooms to clean, dishes to wash, and clothes to iron, but there is simply no time for the children, who spend their hours playing outside or watching TV.

Or what about the counselor who has desperate clients with horrible problems? He sincerely believes that he is needed and is perhaps their only hope. He spends many hours counseling them because of his deep caring and love for others, but back home are a lonely wife and forgotten children.

According to the Bible, these fine people have forgotten their responsibilities. Though they speak of raising children in the right way, beyond the rhetoric and the good intentions, there is only lip service. They have become casual Christians.

Children suffer in three ways. First, they lack necessary instruction. They never have the benefit of learning from their parents what Christians believe, how they should treat one another, or what their responsibilities are in a world that denies God every day.

Second, they lose the opportunity to learn from the example of their parents. They don't see how to live the Christian life, surviving pain, frustration, and loneliness through hope, joy, and peace. They never see an example of how they should raise their families, teach their children, or honor their wife or husband.

Finally, and maybe worst of all, they don't experience the depth of God's love from those who should be the closest to them and best able to express that love and devotion. While each of us has an obligation to bear the witness of Christ to others, parents and children have a unique relationship that provides the most fertile opportunity for such education and training—an opportunity that far too often is not taken seriously.

Perhaps the reason why the casual Christian is so casual in his relationship to God the Father is because of the casual relationship his father had with him. He may simply be expressing what he was first shown.

If that is true, and I believe it is, then the casual Christian, who fails to understand his own beliefs or put into practice what he proclaims with his mouth, will multiply his number each day. He will raise generation after generation of people who carry a false banner and hide behind a façade, a sham, and a lie that they claim is Christianity.

⌒∞⌒

TWELVE

The Christian Home

For many, home refers to a place. For a soldier on foreign soil, it's his native country. For the corporate employee, it may be the town he grew up in. For others, it's the house where they were raised.

But to Christians, home means much more. It isn't an old house, a city, or a country. A Christian home involves people, individual lives with their interaction and growth. For Christians, a home is *the family of God living within the family of man.*

A casual Christian, interested in his own satisfaction, finds his home merely a place to relax and "be himself." It's his refuge from demands and pressures, usually his haven from responsibility.

The Christian home, however, is just the opposite. Here we find the greatest demands, the highest responsibilities, and the deepest pressures. It is center stage for exemplifying and teaching the mysteries of our faith, the place where we lay the foundation for generations to come.

Recently, I read a few newspaper articles that greatly disturbed me. The first involved a violent crime committed by a fourteen-year-old boy. While playing basketball, he didn't feel a younger friend was trying hard enough. At the height of his frustration, he went to a van, pulled out his father's revolver, and shot the boy between the eyes. Returning to the van, he drove home and waited for the police. The boy never showed even the slightest bit of remorse for what he had done.

A second article was about a national survey conducted by the Center for Disease Control in Atlanta, Georgia. According to the study, more than one out of every four teenagers had contemplated suicide as a legitimate solution to their problems. Of those, almost all had developed a specific plan for carrying out their death.

In yet another article, one out of every five high school students admitted to carrying a weapon because they were afraid of being attacked. They did this even knowing they were more likely to be hurt by the very weapon they carried. Also, more than one-half of the students admitted using alcohol, one-third being classified as heavy drinkers. Alcohol and marijuana use were four times higher than the national health objectives. Tobacco and cocaine use were three times higher. All in spite of information given daily through television, schools, and newspapers that such drug and tobacco use are leading causes of death.

Articles such as these lead to an undeniable conclusion: *There's a very serious problem in the home today.* For Christians, the cause lies in a failure to place the proper degree of importance on our witness in the home. However, when we listen to God, we find it to be among the most important areas of our lives.

Go Home

In His travels, Jesus once met a man who was very violent and had done horrible things to himself. People tried to confine him, but he broke the chains and escaped to the tombs, living like a wild animal. Jesus showed great mercy and healed him. As Jesus was about to leave, the man begged to go with Him and be one of His followers. Jesus gave the healed man a more important task: "'Go home to your family and tell them how much the Lord has done for you, and how he has had mercy on you'" (Mark 5:19).

Jesus' command must have stunned this poor man. He had lived a terrible life; deprived of human fellowship and compassion, he'd seen only misery, loneliness, and torment. Now someone had come bringing joy back to his life. With sincere thanks and adoration, he asked to go and be with Jesus. But Jesus said, "No." Instead, He told the man to return to his home, to those same people who bound him in chains, to those same people who left him alone, to those same people who had abandoned him.

Was he to return in triumph for overcoming his illness? Was he to go home to condemn the people for not helping in his time of need? Was he to tell them that they had broken God's commands and displeased Him?

No. Although the man may not have realized it, Jesus was telling him to show the world how special the home is in the family of God and what our responsibilities there are.

Jesus of course wants us to follow Him, but notice that until we are called to a specific ministry, nothing is more important than our responsibility within the home. It is there, with our family, that God wants us to tell of all the things He has done for us and of His tremendous grace in our lives. In our home, God wants us to share His love.

News reports and statistics tell us these instructions are not being carried out. Drug abuse, suicide, and violence—the fact that these not only occur within families but that families are shocked to learn of the occurrence demonstrates the sad degree to which family members don't really know each other. The time we spend with our families is of tremendous importance, but no more so than what we do with that time.

Jesus' first instruction to the healed man was to turn his attention to his own home, to concentrate his efforts on his own family, regardless of how they had acted toward him.

"Go home. Be with your family. Share with them. Tell them about God and His love for you so they might understand the depth of His love for them. Let this be the first thing you do."

The home—the family—is very special in the kingdom of God. It's where we share with those closest to us the depths of who God is and the awesome acts of love He has expressed in our lives.

Tell Them

Jesus' second instruction, "Tell them," appears simple on the surface, but we must carefully consider the words Jesus used. Notice the implied word *you*, so that the instruction would actually be, "You tell them." This is important!

Jesus didn't care what position the man had in the community or his family. We don't know if he was returning to children or a wife, to parents or neighbors. And why is this important? Because the Holy Spirit, in revealing God's Word to us, purposefully makes no distinction. Jesus wanted *this* man to tell what had happened to him specifically. He didn't say, "Go and tell the temple priest so he can tell everyone."

Jesus put the responsibility on the individual to share what God had done for him. He wanted it to be a *personal* testimony.

Far too often we give this job to others. We don't sit down with our families, neighbors, and friends, and tell them, item by item, what God has done in our lives. By our silence, it becomes the work of preachers and ministers.

What's wrong with this picture? Consider the following.

You are watching the six o'clock news and hear a report about a house fire. There was substantial damage and a family was left homeless. They escaped in their pajamas and had to stand in freezing water, but no one was harmed.

Now suppose you are sitting at home when there's a knock on the door. It's a close friend who comes in and, filled with emotion, tells how his house caught on fire last night. He cries as he recalls the irreplaceable, personal things that were lost, including the Christmas presents he and his wife had bought for their children. He describes in detail the intense heat and the suffocating smoke, how he tried to put the fire out but it just got larger, and how difficult it was to wake up one of his sons. Finally, shaking his head, he tells you how thankful he is to God for getting everyone out alive.

Which of these accounts would affect you more? Of course, it would be the second. Someone you actually know and care for is telling of a tremendous event that occurred in his life. It's personal and there's no room for doubt or question.

This is one reason why Jesus told the man to go home and tell his family, and why that same instruction was also meant for each of us. When we share what has happened in our lives, it is personal and real. Those who hear our story are confronted with the truth. When we hear people we don't know, it is easier not to take it as seriously. We think maybe they're exaggerating or just trying to get attention, so we lessen the impact of their story.

But if the person speaking is our mother or father, our son or daughter, our brother or sister, everything takes on a different tone. We know this person well, and we are confronted with a simple choice: Either what has been said is the truth or a lie.

Jesus wants this kind of sharing and interaction in families. He wants us to tell each other what He has done for us. He wants the family to be confronted with His reality.

The Message

So, what exactly are we supposed to say? "Tell them how much the Lord has done for you, and how he has had mercy on you." Pure and simple. "Tell your family about me and how much I love you." Isn't this the message of the gospel? Doesn't this require sharing some of your personal life?

Notice that Jesus wasn't referring to a one-time event. He moves and works in our lives each day. His expressions of love are not momentary, but continuing. Likewise He wants this sharing in the family to be a continuing activity, not just once in a lifetime or only on special occasions. Our memories of times with our families should be filled with the sharing of God in our lives.

The Christian family today experiences many problems and pressures from the world. We worry about our children, a spouse's safety, aging parents, and the rising costs of housing, food, and clothing.

But Jesus says, "Your first concern is to tell your family how much the Lord has done for you and how He has had mercy on you."

What about the monthly mortgage payment? What about our savings? What about the job I may lose?

Jesus says, "Go home and tell them about me."

If we share what God has done for us, our families will grow strong enough to withstand the evil and frustration of this world. God will use this to build a foundation through which we will be prepared for spiritual growth, secure in a relationship based on meaningful prayer, and strengthened in love and encouragement.

cℵ‿

The Christian Parent

So far, we've looked at the responsibilities of family members in general. Now we turn to a special responsibility of every Christian father, mother, and adult who has an influence in the lives of children. "Fathers, do not exasperate your children; instead, bring them up in the training and instruction of the Lord" (Eph. 6:4). "My son, keep your father's commands and do not forsake your mother's teaching" (Prov. 6:20).

When we think of instruction, training, or discipline, we usually focus on the child. He is the recipient of this good work, and there are many verses encouraging him to listen carefully, stay on the right path, and be obedient. But many times we fail to consider the flip side of that coin.

As the above two passages show, there's something else expected by God when it comes to raising children. Parents have a responsibility before God to teach, instruct, and train their children in the lifestyle He has prescribed. In other words, we are to (1) tell our children what it means to be a Christian and (2) be the living example for them to see.

This can be a difficult task, but God never places before us something that cannot be done. In this way, His very command becomes a promise, an assurance that when we are obedient to His will, God Himself will be there working to bring it about.

Remember His promises! He will be with us always, even when it comes to raising our children. We have no need to worry if we turn everything over to Him and let Him be in charge. When we pray in faith and according to His will, all we have to do is ask and it will be done. Raising children as God has instructed not only provides them with a firm spiritual foundation, but it also allows our own faith to grow.

As Christian instructors and examples, we must be constantly aware of three areas that affect how children grow spiritually; if we're to provide sound Christian guidance and training, we cannot overlook them. They are: (1) commitment, (2) communication, and (3) dependence.

Commitment

When Jesus told the healed man to return home and tell what God had done and of His great mercy (see Mark 5:19), Jesus was simply saying, "Tell them how much God loves you."

As we have seen, love is not a warm, fuzzy emotion. God has made it clear that love is based in action. Our love for Him is found in obedience to His commands, and its purest expression is in our desire and efforts to carry them out.

In describing relationships among people, Jesus tells us that love is of the utmost importance. "'A new command I give you: Love one another. As I have loved you, so you must love one another. By this all men will know that you are my disciples, if you love one another'" (John 13:34–35).

The love we are to show is the same kind Jesus has shown us—self-sacrificing for the good of another. And it's not only for the benefit of our Christian brother or sister; it is God's statement to the entire world.

Consider what this means in the context of a family. As a Christian parent, do you really love your child? Is it only a display of emotion that changes with your moods? Do your actions show the love Jesus has described?

When we really love our children, personal desires, wants, and goals are put aside. We focus on the one we love, and that focusing is called commitment.

Jesus said that if we love Him, we will be committed to following and obeying Him. In the same way, if we love our children, we will be committed to them. We will love them with the same love Jesus has shown for us, and we will be willing to lay down our lives for our children. In short, we will be committed to raising our children in the way

God has commanded because we love God and we want to share that love with our children.

Commitment. Though we may sometimes fail and falter, our children will always be able to see God's love through our commitment to God and to them.

Communication

The second area that affects the spiritual growth of children is communication. Unfortunately, it is the most misunderstood. We often fail to see what we are communicating and unknowingly set the stage for the casual Christian to undermine the witness of God's people.

The problem lies in not understanding the many ways we communicate. We may think of the words we choose, the tone of our voice, or the expression on our face, but these are only a part of what communication is all about. Though the Bible contains many passages on speech, God doesn't stop there. He defines communication in a different way: the sharing of our faith (see Philem. 6); the ways of people (see Ps. 37:14); a person's conduct (see Phil. 1:27); and a way of life (see Heb. 13:7).

I believe Peter summed it up perfectly. Communication, after all is said and done, is simply *all that we do* (see 1 Pet. 1:15). Communication involves everything. It's in the words we speak, the expressions on our faces, and the tone of our voices. It is also in the actions we take and the responses we make to life's every situation. This is why the casual Christian is so destructive in the false witness he gives. He communicates different messages. His words and actions don't match.

Those who receive his communication are left only to wonder, "Is this man a liar, a hypocrite, or a fool? One thing's certain. He obviously doesn't believe what he says." And so they walk away, confused and disbelieving.

A casual Christian can have the same effect on children. When he doesn't live the life he claims, if his conduct doesn't support what he says about following Jesus, then he sends conflicting messages. As far as God's kingdom is concerned, he communicates only that something is wrong. Remember what we have said before: What a child believes to be true is formed by what he sees, hears, and experiences.

As Paul says in his letter to Philemon, communication is also a sharing experience, a time of listening as well as speaking. How can we respond if we don't see and hear what's being communicated to us?

As you seek God's guidance in providing the right kind of communication to a child, pray for sensitive ears that hear more than the mere words being spoken. Pray that God will allow you to look into the eyes of a child and understand the depths of his soul. Then take the opportunity to share, preparing him for God's kingdom. "Set an example for the believers in speech, in life, in love, in faith and in purity" (1 Tim. 4:12).

If we strive toward the communication God has commanded, we will certainly find His hand in raising our children.

Dependence

Along with commitment and communication is one more critical ingredient: a clear, unquestioning dependence on God. As committed Christians, we want to know more about God, His love, wisdom, and mercy. We especially want to understand His will for our lives.

A significant aspect of this is the underlying dependence we have on God. We depend on His guidance and direction. We depend on His promises that He will be with us, that we can come to Him in prayer, and that if we do and ask according to His will, we will have what we ask for. We depend on His Word, His mercy, His promise of salvation, and eternal life surrounded by His infinite love.

If we are growing spiritually, we experience God. We draw closer to Him and He draws closer to us, just as He said He would. When that happens, our love for God grows, our relationship with Him becomes more meaningful, and we look to Him more and more for everything in our lives. *We depend on God!*

As we encourage our children in their walk with God, they should witness our dependence on Him. The Bible gives a wonderful example in the life of Noah.

Noah was not a ship builder. He was a farmer, and like any other farmer, he knew how to raise crops. He didn't know a thing about building boats, much less enormous ones.

And yet, God spoke and Noah listened. God told him how evil the world had become and that He would destroy it in a great flood, but He assured Noah that he and his family would be saved. Then God told this farmer, "I want you to build a huge boat."

Noah thoroughly depended on God. First, he depended on His word and assurance of what was about to happen. Second, he depended on His promise that Noah and his family would be protected. Third, he depended on God's instructions to build this ark.

Without question, Noah and his family suffered all kinds of ridicule from those around them. After all, here was a man, a farmer at that, trying to build a boat and not even in the water, but on dry land. Then God instructed Noah to gather all kinds of birds and animals. Again, this wasn't Noah's normal job. He didn't know about all these animals or how to care for them. But he depended on God.

Finally, when the rains came and the land was flooded, Noah, his family, and all the animals were set adrift for more than a year. This is even more amazing when we remember that Noah didn't know how to sail this boat. Yet he still depended on God.

When the rains stopped and the land dried, God spoke again and told Noah that it would be safe for them to leave the boat. Do you remember what Noah did next? He built an altar to God honoring Him for all that had occurred. *Before his family, Noah acknowledged the sovereignty of God and his submission to and dependence on his Lord.*

In this story, we often focus on God's judgment, His awesome power, or His mercy on Noah and his family. But if we read too quickly, we'll miss one of its most important lessons.

During the construction of the ark, the flood, and the many days drifting in the water, Noah looked in only one direction. He looked to God for everything—for his assurance, his guidance, his sustenance, his safety, and his life. And through it all were the children. They saw their father in total submission to God. They witnessed his complete and undeniable dependence on his Lord.

Through Noah's dependence, God was glorified before Noah's children. They were given the opportunity to see God in all of His power, authority, majesty, judgment, mercy, grace, and love. *Because of their father's desire to depend only on his Lord, they experienced God too!*

Sharing the Experience

This can also happen today. When Christian parents rely on God for everything in their lives, they send a powerful message to their children: God is real; God is alive; God is active; He can be trusted to take care of us; His way is best; He loves us; and He is worthy to be praised.

How can this message be sent? First, parents and children can pray together. Each day children should hear their parents' confession that God is in charge of their lives, that Jesus is their Lord, and that their desire is to carry out His will. They should hear words of praise, thanks for God's love, and earnest requests for direction.

Second, parents and children can study God's Word. Together they can grow in their understanding and knowledge of God. Together they can seek His guidance for life's many questions and trials.

Third, they can share with each other the events of the day—what they saw, what happened to them and to others, and how they responded. Parents may not always have a ready response, but they can use this time to reflect on what a Christian should say or do.

And fourth, parents can use themselves as examples, showing not only the good, but also the bad. We often learn more from another's mistakes than triumphs, and children need to know that their parents have flaws, too. More importantly, they should see their parents working through such flaws out of a deep love for God and a desire to follow Christ.

The key is sharing. As Christian parents commit their lives to God; if they acknowledge their responsibilities to instruct and train their children in the Christian lifestyle; if they communicate with their children, speaking and living the truths and commands of our faith; and if they base their commitment and communication on a complete and utter dependence on God, then their children will grow into the stature of men and women who love, obey, and serve God as true witnesses of who He really is. Their homes will be founded on the love of God, and their relationships with God and each other will grow and strengthen.

It will happen! When these children look at their parents, they won't see just their mother or father. They will see and experience God in their parents' lives. What greater gift could we give our children than the opportunity to know Him?

V

The Witness
At Work

Do not wear yourself out to get rich; have the wisdom to show restraint.

Proverbs 23:4

❧

The Work Shift

Each week we go through transformations that can change our entire personalities. We may not even notice the movement from one to another, like chameleons altering colors to suit our changing environment. But the fact that these changes occur says a lot about who we are as Christians and where we are in our spiritual walk.

One transformation is the *Pious Period*, which occurs as we walk through the church doors. It usually only happens once or twice a week.

The second occurs much more often. In many ways it is the single most destructive factor hindering the spread of the gospel and the witness of Christianity. This almost daily transformation is the *Work Shift*.

When we discussed the family, we noted that the home is one place where others see us for who we really are. The guards are let down and we can just be ourselves.

This changes dramatically when it's time to go to work. Why? Because, to a certain degree, others require it. For example, in some businesses men must wear white shirts and women wear dresses. In others, they have to wear vests with the company logo or uniforms with their names on them.

The changes aren't limited to clothing. In some businesses, male employees can't have mustaches or beards. A few sports teams have rules about the length of a person's hair. If we work for these businesses, we must change our appearance in a more permanent way.

However, all of the changes in the *Work Shift* aren't the result of company rules or policies. Most occur simply because of what we believe others expect from us and what we expect of ourselves.

My own profession is a great example. How many people, struggling with a legal problem, expect to walk into a lawyer's office to find someone in Bermuda shorts, leather sandals, and a T-shirt proclaiming worldwide protection for large aquatic mammals? No one.

Right or wrong, we expect to see a person dressed in a pin-striped suit with coordinating dress shirt, conservative tie, and laced, wingtip shoes. When our expectations are met, we feel more comfortable. Although there is no dress code for the average lawyer, he or she simply reacts to what the public expects or demands.

The approval of others can dictate the manner of our dress, actions, and speech, and to achieve it, we often adopt an image. In the safety of our home, we may allow our true selves to come out of hiding; but as we take our morning shower, put on our clothes, and hurry out the door, we become a different person, fully capable of acting and speaking in ways we may not want our friends in church to see or hear.

We make this transformation effortlessly, without a thought or concern. We have gone to work, where we will spend most of our waking hours and have the greatest opportunity to affect the lives of those around us. Yet no one knows who we really are.

Image and Actions

There's an ad campaign that uses an interesting marketing approach. It never refers to quality or price. Instead it makes one simple statement: *Image is everything.*

The typical business manufactures an image for the public to see, molding it into a form that will attract attention, praise, and respect. But often the image is only an empty shell, having no relation to reality or truth. For example, many businesses claim to support "traditional values," such as quality and reasonable prices. Yet what they really promote is the *image* of having such values, not the values themselves.

Sadly, we not only participate in such deception, we sometimes encourage it. The promotion of an image is easily found in the players of the *Work Shift,* where the primary goal in business is not to offer a good product or service, but to be number one. No compromises are offered and no excuses accepted. Because society has adopted this philosophy as a natural part of the business world, all rules have been set aside. Everything is allowed short of illegal acts, or I should say, short of being caught.

Savings and Loans, once enormous financial institutions, lie in ruins, the result of greedy men and women who shamelessly violated the law to pave their way to the top. Securities firms, obligated to guard secret information, give in to the temptation to get easy money. Laws are broken and confidences breached. A man's word means little if anything, becoming just a part of the game to secure the deal and nothing more.

The Decline of Integrity

There was a time when a person's character depended on the integrity of his word. As a young man fresh out of law school, I had the pleasure of practicing law in Fayette County, at that time a rural area of Georgia. Although trained in the intricacies of contracts and agreements, I discovered that many of the fine people there simply didn't have time to bother with mounds of paperwork and confusing language. Deals were often concluded with the shake of a hand. It meant something to give someone your word.

I remember once advising a client that he didn't have to do some task because the agreement wasn't in writing as required by law. He looked me dead in the eye and said, "You don't understand. My word is the most important thing I have and the most important thing I can give. My word is what I am. If my word means nothing, then I'm nothing."

His integrity was important to him, and you could see it in how he treated others. You could depend on what he said. If he committed to something, he followed it through even when circumstances had changed to his disadvantage. The man had integrity, *and it meant everything to him!* Jesus explained it this way: "'The good man brings good things out of the good stored up in him, and the evil man brings evil things out of the evil stored up in him. But I tell you that men will have to give account on the day of judgment for every careless word they have spoken. For by your words you will be acquitted, and by your words you will be condemned'" (Matt. 12:35–37).

As the casual Christian does business, he ignores Jesus' teachings. Unlike my client so long ago, he puts integrity aside in his struggle to the top of the heap.

This is often seen in contract negotiations, where lying is the number one tool of the trade. Of course, we don't call it lying. Under the law it's often referred to as *puffery,* an act of exaggeration found to be common and even expected in a given industry, such as car sales. In court, this exaggeration takes on a new name. Now we call it *malicious fraud* or *insignificant misrepresentation,* depending on which side you're on.

Though I hate to say it, the courts themselves provide the opportunity for more lying and cheating. Why? Because integrity is not the focus of their attention. Instead, harm is. The fact that someone has lied will not necessarily void a transaction. It doesn't matter that you would never have done business with a liar. The court's only interest is whether there has been significant harm resulting from the *misrepresentation.* The court won't even use the word *lie.*

The Advancement of Business

Our society has come to define "doing business" in a way that condones lying and breaking one's word. We foster a process that can have only one result: Integrity takes a back seat to the advancement of business.

The "advancement of business" centers on the promotion of the business itself, that drive to be number one. For this reason, a large company will acquire a smaller one and then bankrupt it, regardless of lost jobs, in order to get certain tax benefits. Businesses break contracts if they believe that, in the long run, they'll be better off financially. Companies illegally dump hazardous wastes to avoid the high costs of properly disposing of the materials, even though such actions endanger the lives of men, women, and children.

This drive to the top causes people to spy on each other, steal trade secrets, and divulge confidential information in an attempt to crush the competition. Some businesses spend more time and effort trying to destroy each other than to improve themselves.

How does this relate to Christians, particularly the casual Christian? Many of those who *misrepresent* their position or omit vital information in business deals also teach Sunday School, chair the finance committee, and organize church bazaars. They say they're Christians, yet fail to give that claim any substance.

The casual Christian takes his two-faced lifestyle developed in the home and perfects it in the business world. The façade of Christianity, so important to him in other areas, is now a detriment and fades from view. Without a thought or a care, he dons a "business" image as though it were a change of clothes, quickly forgetting that he sometimes claims to be Christian.

It is ironic that a "business" image is given such importance while those who maintain it often neglect the image they reserve for themselves. This sends a conflicting message to nonbelievers. In their search for truth, they find confusion which causes them to distrust the true Christian witness and the good news of Jesus Christ.

This makes our job more difficult and more important. It's more difficult because we have a new barrier to overcome, one built with the misconceptions and hypocrisy of the casual Christian. But it's also more important. In this growing darkness of confusion and lies, Christ's light that shines in us must be even clearer to show the true way.

Christians can meet this challenge by encouraging one another as we face the hostile environment of the business world. Changes in how a business handles its affairs don't come easily or quickly. Frustration and disappointment are common. However, a business reflects the conduct of its employees, and our strategy should be to focus our efforts there, in the one-on-one encounters we have every day. As we'll see, the relationships among employees provide our foremost battleground in bringing the true Christian witness to this arena.

Down the Ladder

Most of us like to think that through the course of time, we've become more intelligent, fair minded, and loftier in purpose than our predecessors. We point to our government by the people and for the people and speak of social reform and civil rights. When it comes to business, we claim to be devoted to a system that challenges and selects people on the basis of their skill, expertise, and qualifications. But is this really true?

The Truth of Discrimination

In this country, we have many employment laws which prohibit discrimination on the basis of race, sex, age, national origin, and creed. Unfortunately, the high costs of complicated lawsuits, the tedious government bureaucracy required before seeking court action, and the fear of losing your job while the issue is being raised combine effectively to allow discrimination to continue.

In the meantime, the casual Christian either joins in or keeps quiet. After all, "this is business and you have to play by the rules." His Christian values become lost in a world where the goals of business outweigh the welfare of another human being. He seeks only his own satisfaction, never giving a thought to the plight of his neighbor.

Discrimination is an important issue for every Christian. Within its dark shadow lie two thieves: hatred and indifference. They rob men and women of happiness, security, and hope.

Race discrimination is usually associated with hatred. Many of us have seen employers refuse to hire someone because of his color. We've heard the racial slurs and derogatory jokes. We've watched as many stay in poorly paying jobs with no hope of advancement.

Yet hatred can be found in all forms of discrimination. In a sex discrimination case, a woman was denied a promotion and forced to resign because her supervisor didn't approve of women holding her position. In his anger, he circulated false stories about her character and morals. After she left her job, no one would hire her because of the lies.

In another case, a sixty-one-year-old man, after having the same job for twenty years and receiving many citations for excellent work, was told he couldn't do the job and was fired. During the trial, his supervisor couldn't produce evidence of poor work, but did admit to being angry with the company's policy of keeping older employees while many younger people needed jobs.

Equal to hatred in its effect is indifference. Regardless of qualification or effort, decisions are made on personal preferences, such as feeling more comfortable with a particular race, age, or sex, or choosing on the basis of friendship or personal gain. As it concerns the victim of discrimination, there's no anger, only indifference.

The casual Christian is quickly caught in this snare because discrimination supports his basic desire to seek his own satisfaction. He may even try to defend such actions by arguing he had no choice if he wanted to keep his job. Still this is just choosing self over others.

God will never direct us to do something wrong in order to accomplish something we believe to be right.

Discrimination to save our jobs? Never! God doesn't promise us an easy road, only His love, presence, peace, and joy. But the casual Christian, who hides behind a façade of Christianity, wants more. He has forgotten, ignored, or never learned Jesus' command to put others ahead of himself and love them.

Discrimination affects our Christian witness. If we discriminate, our actions become examples for others. The lost see hatred and indifference instead of God's love. Hypocrisy leaps to the forefront, and our Lord is made to look like a fool.

Discrimination doesn't stop there either. Because it is the child of hatred and indifference, it will also affect other areas of our lives. For example, when people of other races or countries move into our neighborhoods, we often fail to welcome them. We may never ask if they are

Christians or invite them to church. If they come anyway, we may "forget" to sit with them in "our" worship service or invite them back.

Instead, many of us panic, quickly selling our houses and moving away, even if it takes much longer to get to work and doubles our monthly payments. We may even silently leave our churches for others that are "less threatened" and lose friendships that have lasted for years, sometimes without saying goodbye.

What has the casual Christian accomplished here? He's taken discrimination into his home and his church. He's developed assumptions based on someone's color or native country. He's become the agent for hatred and indifference.

Discrimination can't be confined. If allowed, it will spread into every area of our lives. With it grows the deceptively dangerous attitude of indifference, an even greater problem in our society than any attitude of hate.

Hatred is an intense emotion, easy to identify. We can see it in a person's face or hear it in his speech. It is present in riots, murders, rapes, and war. Even though the Bible says God hates certain things, we choose to regard all hatred as being wrong for "civilized people."

Indifference, however, is subtle, easily hidden by false gestures and insincere concern. For example, a city announced its intent to better its community by controlling local peddlers, requiring them to register and carry a license, but the truth showed something different. Big business and the tourist industry weren't concerned about peddlers in their city. They were concerned about the public appearance of homeless men, women, and children. The homeless didn't project the right kind of image, and the city wanted them removed. The actual plight of the homeless was ignored. In this subtle way, the city showed its indifference for those in need.

Indifference has grown substantially in the business world. There have always been rough times with layoffs, cutbacks in production, and business closings. Yet today there's a strong and disturbing force: the consuming drive to be number one. This obsession has taken on such proportions that the welfare of employees is deliberately ignored. Businesses are so preoccupied with their own advancement that the very people who provided the foundation for the company's present success are deemed to be standing in the way of its future. No thought is given to the fact that without them there would have been no future at all.

Simply put, businesses have reached the point where they don't respect or care for their own employees. And yet, they have the gall to demand loyalty.

I once saw a video that a major corporation sent to its employees. According to the tape, the company was in a difficult situation and because of this predicament, it was necessary to reduce its work force by several thousand—in eight months! The reduction would come through early retirement and terminations.

It was the reasons for this action that caught my attention: (1) for the company to remain the leader in its field and (2) for its stockholders to make more money. The battle cry "for the good of the company" echoed throughout the program. No mention was made of improving services or products. It was not disclosed if the stockholders were making a current profit. Instead, it simply called for company loyalty, asking all employees to make this sacrifice "for the good of the company."

There were other things the tape didn't disclose. Some time later I discovered that choosing early retirement also meant agreeing not to work for a competitor. To top it off, only the company could determine who was a competitor. Perhaps the most ridiculous part was that these added conditions weren't disclosed until *after* the employee chose to retire.

This hardly seems to be looking out for the employee. After being trained and uniquely suited to a particular industry, he's told he can't use those same skills again if he elects early retirement. If he chooses not to retire, he stands to be laid off anyway. Indifference rules. The promotion of an artificial entity is placed over the welfare of the very people who give it life.

Unfortunately, the casual Christian doesn't see this or, at most, believes he is unable to do anything. Either way, he is so convinced that business must be separate from his "Christian life," that he can't accept his own hypocrisy or feel the conflict.

Supervisor and Staff

Another area greatly affected by the casual Christian is the relationship among employees. Businesses, after all, involve many who hold a variety of beliefs as well as those who believe nothing at all. Often the Christian may not influence the overall business, but in the relationships among employees, everything is on a more personal level.

In the relationship of a supervisor and his staff, the effect of a casual Christian can be devastating. As a supervisor, he usually has the attention and the initial respect of employees. What a wonderful time to be an example of Christ and share with others. Unfortunately, this seldom occurs. Believing his "Christian life" can be separate from the business world, he may ignore Christ altogether or hide behind a façade of Christianity, making his own rules for how to live and work. Ultimately, he will do whatever makes him the most satisfied and comfortable.

For these reasons, he often becomes the object of scorn and ridicule. He drives others hard, demanding a lot of work and ridiculous timetables. His staff seldom sees their families and often works under stress. But for the casual Christian, these are necessary sacrifices. After all, "it's just part of the job."

Many of us have tremendous work loads from time to time. However, it's important to understand the effect a casual Christian has in this situation.

The typical employee will have many different attitudes. He may feel loyalty toward or disinterest in the company. He may learn to trust others or always protect himself. He may even develop attitudes of life as a whole based on how he finds himself treated. More importantly, if he works for a casual Christian who merely projects an image of Christianity, he will definitely develop attitudes about him. These may develop into beliefs which shape his overall attitude toward Christianity.

Consider the supervisor who preaches the hard work ethic and drives his staff to produce new products. What attitudes are formed when they learn that their trusted supervisor, who spent little time on the project himself, has taken sole credit for their ideas? Of course, they are quite negative: He can't be trusted; he lies and cheats; he puts himself before others; and so forth.

Now, what if they know he goes to church and is a deacon or elder? If the employees are not Christian or are young in their spiritual growth, the results can be terrible. *The actions of their supervisor can become the starting point of what they believe about Christians in general.*

Throughout his life, a person is observed by those around him as definite impressions are made about his character, beliefs, and faith. A significant difference must be noted here. The Christian cares about his witness to the world. The casual Christian, when all is said and done, cares only about himself. He tries to play down his influence by claiming everyone must study the Bible and draw their own conclusions, but he ignores Jesus' direction and caution that we are the light of the world.

Young Christians, learning from his example, are led to believe that Christian life can be separate from life in this world and that such double standards are acceptable. Non-Christians see his behavior and add to their reasons for not believing the truth of the Bible.

Because so many never read God's Word or understand what it has to say, our example becomes their first source for the truth. This is important for us to remember, for we may be the only example of Christ they have ever seen.

∾⬥∾

Employee to Employee

In business the casual Christian has his greatest influence in the relationships among his peers. Even though he may not have automatic power, immediate attention, or initial respect, he does have greater freedom. He can be more relaxed and just one of the guys. This freedom gives him the opportunity to create a false sense of power, authority, and respect.

At times the drive to surpass others is so strong that he will lie, cheat, and steal his way to the top, but these are usually rare attempts that become widely known. His primary tool is very destructive and also the most subtle: the power of speech.

Through what we say, we can directly influence the thoughts, opinions, and actions of others. We can encourage or destroy, show our love or our hate. Most importantly, we can give validity to our claim to be Christian or prove it to be a joke. This power is usually expressed in three distinct ways: criticism, gossip, and profanity.

Criticism

Criticism comes in different forms. When given out of real concern and intended to help, it is constructive criticism. We applaud those who are bold enough to offer such criticism and those wise enough to listen.

Unfortunately, the casual Christian often uses criticism only as a means of expressing his dislike, frustration, and anger. It's not intended to build up but to tear down.

For example, a fellow employee develops a new way to do some necessary task. The casual Christian jumps on it in a heartbeat. It is more important for him to say that it won't work or to point out problems than to take the time to analyze it. Why? Because deep down he doesn't care about the other person or even "the good of the company." By criticizing, he feels important in appearing to be an authority or a significant contributor. When the casual Christian reacts this way, there's only one focus—himself. The feelings of another are never considered.

Now some may argue this isn't his fault because such behavior is expected, if not demanded, by the employer. "The business world is based on the survival of the fittest. If you can't take the heat, get out of the kitchen. After all, that's how business operates."

After representing many different businesses, I agree with these statements—to a point. The business world does foster and reward this type of behavior. However, our choice to be the aggressor and unduly criticize is wrong. Regardless of what may be said, we alone make the final decision to participate, joining with the ways of this world. When we do, we ignore the teachings of Christ in dealing with others. We choose not to encourage, but to frustrate.

Gossip

With destructive criticism comes its natural companion, gossip. The two work well together as the casual Christian seeks to feel important and advance his own causes at the expense of others. The apostle Paul certainly doesn't put it in high company: "For I am afraid that when I come I may not find you as I want you to be. . . . I fear that there may be quarreling, jealousy, outbursts of anger, factions, slander, gossip, arrogance and disorder" (2 Cor. 12:20).

Yet we rush to gossip as though it were a favorite sport. We even condone it among certain people, such as women and the elderly, claiming the poor dears just can't help themselves. Then we make certain we never face the mirror as we join in.

Gossip is simply idle chatter that serves no beneficial purpose. Many gossip for the enjoyment of it, playing "I know something you don't know" and then telling all to prove that they do. Yet no thought is given to the possibility that they may be spreading something that is untrue or something that increases the shame of another person.

And what about the casual Christian? Remember the premise under which this fellow operates in the business world: Christian life is a separate matter and can't be allowed to interfere in his business affairs. Also remember the motive for his actions: self-satisfaction.

With this premise and motive forming the basis for his actions and attitudes, it's no wonder he finds nothing wrong with a little idle gossip. We can hardly be surprised when gossip fills coffee breaks, business luncheons, the company party, and every other spare moment in which employees come together.

While a few would rather read a book, scan the latest news, or even discuss religion, isn't it true that they are ostracized for the most part? Sure, those topics are okay, but if you don't talk about the real issues of the day, such as Dave's lack of taste in clothes, Mary's poor work, or Brenda's upcoming divorce, you're just not with it.

The fact is these are usually not issues that *concern* us. They're issues that *interest* us. Such discussions seldom carry any intent to help, guide, or encourage. They do, however, meet one major desire: They keep us satisfied. We're in the know, perhaps a part of the elite who really see what's going on, and that makes us feel important.

Gossip is also an easy way to undermine and destroy. Through its door, we can vent anger, seek revenge, or prevent someone from getting ahead. The beauty of it is that we can even be telling the truth. We don't have to make anything up; all we have to do is spread the information.

Through gossip, it becomes more difficult to find the truth as each repeated story becomes more vague and the facts more distorted. The retelling becomes a shadow of the truth and in that shadow, anger and disdain continue, while love and reconciliation reach an impasse. "A gossip separates close friends. . . . A fool finds no pleasure in understanding but delights in airing his own opinions. . . . A gossip betrays a confidence. . . . Without gossip a quarrel dies down. . . . A man who lacks judgment derides his neighbor, but a man of understanding holds his tongue" (Prov. 16:28; 18:2; 20:19; 26:20; 11:12).

Is it really all that bad? Can it be wrong when it's just meant in fun and especially when we're telling the truth? Yes, and it's even worse, because God said, "Don't do it" (see 1 Pet. 3:8–12).

Profanity

One of the most demanding jobs I had working my way through college was as a meter reader. I was chased by every dog in DeKalb County and suffered through all kinds of weather, but God used it to open my eyes to those around me. I walked through areas that were dirt poor, where people lacked running water and paved streets. I also worked in neighborhoods where the servants escorted me through the mansion. In some communities, I had the only white face for miles. In others, I was the only one who could speak clear English.

Through this, God taught me something very important. It's not the neighborhood, the size of a house, or the color of your skin that is the final determination of who you are. It's what is on the inside. Men and women come out of poverty and find success. Illiterate parents have children who become novelists. Communities rich in folklore and tradition produce doctors, professors, and lawyers. Influences on the outside affect us only as we ultimately allow them to.

When it comes to profanity, again the choice is ours. Gentle speaking people as well as the profane cross all boundaries, income levels, neighborhoods, ethnic groups, and races. But why do some use profanity at all?

Profanity is a powerful tool often used to intimidate others, and it is very effective in providing a false sense of importance, acceptance, and authority. There are two ways in which profanity is most commonly used: in expressions of anger and in casual conversation. Let's first look at anger.

In old movies or TV shows, expressions of anger were suppressed. If an actor hit his hand with a hammer, he was usually tight-lipped. Today things have changed, and we hear plenty of profanity. Now we're told that stories should depict real life in every way, including speech. Though shocked at first, we have come to accept profanity as correct expressions of anger that depict how we really feel and how we might act in similar situations.

Through what the media has offered, many have adopted this "freer" speech as a *natural* outburst of human emotion and are no longer shocked at the most vulgar forms of profanity. We accept it as a part of life, and by our silence we give approval.

Over the years, I've had many opportunities to observe how business people handle their anger, and I've noticed something quite interesting. Those who control their anger are effective in analyzing problems, developing sound solutions, working with others in stressful situations, and achieving results. They remain calm in spite of the storm, giving them a chance to reflect, study, and plan.

Who are these people? Generally they are men and women with beliefs and faiths that teach self-control. Many are devout Hindus, Moslems, and Buddhists. Others follow strict practices of meditation seeking inner peace. Some find direction in New Age philosophies that speak of god-powers which they claim inhabit every man and woman.

Sadly, it has also been my experience that few of these people claim to be Christian. The typical Christian I meet in the business world is often out of control and vents his anger through a stream of profanity, usually directing it at those around him.

Once, while waiting to meet with another attorney, I suddenly heard a telephone being thrown across a room; a barrage of curses flew from his private office. His secretary nervously laughed and told me he was under a lot of pressure and wasn't always like this. However, I found it occurred with some frequency and without any regard for who might be listening.

I also noticed something else over the next few weeks. His use of profanity was so common it became a part of his everyday speech in casual conversation, jokes, descriptions of people, and discussions of events, even a part of his sighs.

It is also important to point out that he was an active member of his church, a deacon, a leader of his congregation, and a teacher. He was a frequent speaker on Christian causes and beliefs.

The sad truth about people like this man is they believe they are better than the casual Christian, but it's almost impossible to see the difference. They are blind to reality because they are comfortable where they are. The walls of their façade have become quite strong.

The effect in the business world is clearly demonstrated by this example. This man's employees once admitted that if he hadn't said he was a Christian, they never would have known. One of his clients even expressed genuine surprise when told that her attorney was a Christian.

Do you see what has happened here? The witness is lost! There's no light for others to see.

There is great power in the written word, having a profound effect on thoughts, beliefs, and ideas. A document can be studied and analyzed, passed around for review and comment, and revised to reflect new opinions.

Just as the written word is powerful to future generations, thinkers, and planners, the spoken word is equally powerful in its effect on the present. Carelessly spoken words can hurt, anger, defame, and destroy.

Often the casual Christian never considers the effect his profanity may have. Sometimes it lets him be just one of the guys, while at other times it gives him a sense of authority. Through profanity, he shows the world he can say what he wants and that he alone is the master of his life.

But God tells us, "Reckless words pierce like a sword" (Prov. 12:18). They strike the one who utters them, injuring, if not destroying, his ability to witness in this world. Who will believe someone who refuses to follow what he claims to be true? No one. How can the world believe what he says about Christ? *It can't, and it won't.*

In Matthew 15:18, Jesus says that "'the things that come out of the mouth come from the heart.'" Words of hate, anger, and profanity reflect the evil present in our lives; but there is something critical here that we can't afford to miss, something so simple that many rush past without taking the time to notice. Jesus isn't telling us anything new. He's reminding us of something we already know. "If anyone considers himself religious and yet does not keep a tight rein on his tongue, he deceives himself and his religion is worthless" (James 1:26).

What an individual says and how he speaks go a long way in telling others what kind of a person he is. The life of one who claims to be a Christian is constantly under the watchful and critical eyes of an unfriendly world. In the workplace, those around him will soon discover whether or not he's a liar. "A fool's mouth is his undoing, and his lips are a snare to his soul" (Prov. 18:7).

God takes this very seriously. *So should we!*

∽∞∾

Image and Perception

It was still early morning when Bob walked briskly out of his home and opened the door to his company car. He tossed his briefcase in the back, sat in the soft leather seat, and started the engine. Noticing a knocking noise, he made a mental note to have the company's garage pool check it out.

They never can seem to get this thing fixed, he thought to himself.

Bob had been given the use of a car by his employer about six years earlier and received a new one every two years thereafter. Though he had never given much thought and attention to his personal car, now he wanted to make sure that everything appeared to be in perfect working order.

As Bob made his predawn, two-hour pilgrimage to his office, he reviewed his daily schedule recorded in the company notebook computer, checking on the numerous meetings and deadlines reserved for his attention. He then reached for his mobile phone and called his office.

"Ann, please change my 3:00 meeting with marketing to Sunday at 10:00 A.M.," he instructed his secretary's voice mail, "and set up a conference call for 1:30 today with Pete over in Operations."

After battling the early morning traffic, Bob finally wheeled into the company parking garage and parked in a space that bore his name. He then gathered his computer and briefcase, as well as a few memos he had managed to write on his way in, and made his way to the private entrance. Once there, he pulled out his coded key pass and slid it into the electronic scanner.

CODE NOT ACCEPTED ran across the message panel.

Strange, Bob thought. *They must have changed the access codes and forgot to give me a new keycard.*

Bob knocked on the door and got the attention of a security guard.

"Yes, Mr. Johnson. Forgot your card?" the guard asked cheerfully.

"No," Bob responded curtly. "Apparently something's wrong with mine. Must have been damaged somehow."

Once the guard opened the door, Bob entered and continued to his private office on the fifty-second floor. The office was quite spacious and well-decorated, proof to himself that he had succeeded over the years. On the walls hung certificates commemorating Bob on ten, twenty, and thirty years of service. There were plaques recognizing his efforts in achieving record sales for his company, as well as a few thanking him for contributing to various community efforts.

Bob walked around his desk, put his briefcase on the floor, and sat in his executive chair. Spinning around, he looked out over the city's horizon, just now brightening with the approaching sun.

Looking back toward his desk computer, he noticed a message had been sent through the company's E-mail system. Entering the appropriate commands, he brought the message to the screen: "Bob, please see me as soon as you come in. Ed."

Though only half Bob's age and just ten years out of college, Ed was the regional vice president and Bob's immediate supervisor.

"Must be a problem with the Camden account," he said to himself.

Bob hurried down the hall and took the elevator to the next floor where he continued on to Ed's office.

Peering in the doorway, he saw Tom, Ed's assistant, sitting in the corner. "Ed, did you want to see me?"

Ed looked up from a stack of files on his desk. "Come on in," he replied wearily. "Have a seat over here, and would you close the door please?"

For the next fifteen minutes, Bob listened as Ed, in a deathly monotone, read from a sheet of paper . . . how Bob had been a valued and loyal employee, how his many years of service had been very appreciated and an inspiration to many, how the company had been through some rough years and had not made the profits it should have, how the officers and directors had a responsibility to maximize those profits for the stockholders, how it had become necessary to downsize the company's management, and how . . . Bob no longer had a job.

As Ed read the company's instructions, Bob sat in silence with his head in his hands, too stunned to speak.

Ed finally placed the piece of on his desk.

"Now, Bob, security being what it is, I know you will understand that we are only following procedures, but I will need you to clean out your desk and vacate the building. Your car has already been picked up, so you will have to make other arrangements to get home. Please don't try to access anything in the computer as we have already deleted your password. The notebook computer issued to you should be left in the office with your car keys, the building keycard, and all files, documents, memos, and notes of any nature related to our work here."

Bob raised his head, his eyes fixed on the floor. "How much time do I have?"

"Twenty minutes."

In a few short minutes, everything that counted in Bob's life, everything that meant he had made it, that he was a success and a person to be reckoned with, was taken away from him. No company car or mobile phone. No computer or secretary. No crucial meetings or last minute conferences. No office. No job. For the first time in his life, he saw himself as having nothing—and being nothing.

How we see ourselves, to a great degree, determines how we define such things as success, comfort, and security. These in turn shape our perceptions of where we find ourselves in the great scheme of things. The problem lies in which reference book we use.

For example, much has been published attempting to solve the problem of low self-esteem, and many like Bob rush to embrace such teachings. The popular "solution" is simple: Each person must believe he is important because he is. If that sounds like it's going in circles, that's because it is. The reason we are important is because we say we are? In such a theory, we become our own authority, and that's where the conflict arises.

If a person has low self-esteem, he thinks he's not important. He may lack self-confidence or feel totally dependent on others. To say that he should suddenly regard himself as important suggests the existence of some internal switch that just isn't there.

Other "authorities" say to tap into an eternal power that, they claim, lies within every living creature, a power that joins them with the universe and which they can control. This New Age philosophy has a strong influence in business today, although it's usually hidden by less obvious descriptions and titles.

The Bible, on the other hand, teaches that each person has his own significance and importance in the kingdom of God. Each individual is precious to God, and His relationship with us is on an individual basis. God's Word also teaches that we are all a part of the body of Christ. While each has his own gifts and talents, no one is higher or more important than another. This is even true in regard to our sins. We have all fallen short, but as equals, we are to work together for the glory of God, not for the praise of others.

The casual Christian has a difficult time with this. In business, he's told the cream will rise to the top. Everything and everybody are rated in terms of importance. Though much may be said of the outstanding efforts of the masses, it is a select few at the top of the heap who get the most money, best offices, luxury cars, and expensive homes. The casual Christian buys into this rating system and, as a result, sees himself in terms not as defined by God, but as defined by the world.

For example, what do people ask when they meet each other? "So, where are you working now?" "Are you still with so and so?" "What are you doing these days?"

We are caught up with each other's employment, employer, and position because we subconsciously use these to define who we are. "Senior vice president of International Big Company." Has a nice ring, doesn't it? True or not, it gives the impression of financial success, importance, and authority. In the same way, so does "Pastor of Huge Church with Lots of People in It."

We are so conditioned to this way of thinking that we fail to ask the really important questions. "How's your health?" "Is the family doing all right?" "Have you been able to handle the stress?" "Has so-and-so become a Christian?" And so on.

It may sound harsh, but these questions are seldom asked by the casual Christian because he really doesn't care. How another person is doing isn't as significant as how *he* is doing. His success defines who he is, and if he loses that job or the business fails, there's nothing left in his world to give life meaning. In his eyes, he's become . . . nothing.

As a result, he constantly compares himself with others, and the objects of his comparison, such as salary, title, company car, designer suits, and so on, become his idols. If he doesn't have them, he strives to attain them. If he gets his desires, he wants better ones than others may have. Success, importance, and personal achievement ultimately mean nothing more than having the key to the executive restroom.

Jesus says that if we love Him, we will obey Him and be willing to give up all material possessions to follow His will. Don't desire what another has. Don't be jealous or envious because someone has more than you. "For where you have envy and selfish ambition, there you find disorder and every evil practice" (James 3:16). "Those who live like this will not inherit the kingdom of God" (Gal. 5:21).

The casual Christian hears the words on Sunday morning but fails to understand. He leaves the church content with himself and his ambitions, driving a car with a bumper sticker that tells the world of his commitment: He who dies with the most toys—wins!

⟡

The Business Mission Field

What takes priority in the life of a Christian? Regardless of anything going on around you, regardless of age, sex, race, national origin, the size of your income or house, what's the number one priority in your life?

For the casual Christian, it is seeking his own satisfaction. He acts the way he wants. His life is *self*-centered. But if we're not to be like him, does our priority lie in others? Should the benefit, care, prosperity, and well-being of those around us be the number-one priority in our lives?

No! It is important to stay focused here. Our priority is not in caring for others. Because of this attitude, many Christians are involved in great works of charity and good will but remain light years from what they should be doing. Just like the casual Christian, they live with misplaced priorities.

Setting the Priority

For Christians, there is only one priority: to obey God. Sounds simple enough, but it requires great effort. We need to draw closer to God, have a meaningful relationship with Him, seek His will in all things, and then act on what He directs us to do. As the apostle John points out, our love for God can only be demonstrated through our obedience to His will.

So what does this have to do with the Christian in the business world? *Everything!*

The work place is one of the most fertile grounds for the Christian witness. In this setting we meet many different people and in a personal way—face to face. Working side by side, our opportunity to witness is tremendous. Before we can witness, however, our priorities must be in order. We have to decide that, above all else, we will obey God and follow His leading.

Understand what is at stake here! If obeying God is the priority in our lives, then we will follow Him *even at the risk of losing customers, clients, patients, promotions, raises, bonuses—even at the risk of losing our jobs!* There can be no waffling. Either something is a priority or it's not. Either obeying is the most important thing in our lives or it's nothing more than a lukewarm New Year's resolution.

If obeying God is the priority, then, like Noah, we'll depend on Him for everything, because we know we can't look to the world for anything. As Jesus tells us, following Him won't give us a particularly pleasant time in the world. "'I have told you these things, so that in me you may have peace. In this world you will have trouble'" (John 16:33).

Then why do it if we're going to have so much trouble? Why not just live a peaceful life, never get in anybody's way, and let our religion be a *private* affair? Because such an attitude is self-centered and contrary to a true Christian witness. Remember, God defines a Christian as one who believes Jesus is the Son of God and applies His teachings and commands in his life (see John 3:16); refuses his own desires, takes up the cause of Christ and follows Jesus (see Luke 9:23); loves others in the same self-sacrificing way Jesus showed for us in His life (see John 13:34); and loves God and is loved by God (see John 14:21).

In this sense, we don't set the priority; God does. He alone makes the rules, and obedience to Him is the key. "'If you love me, you will obey what I command'" (John 14:15).

To be a Christian means that we are to obey—even at work.

The Nature of Our Witness

A friend once confided that she had a problem being a Christian at work. I was surprised because she loved God and devoutly served His kingdom. Yet she was having serious doubts about herself.

Her concern arose from two separate incidents. The first involved a promotion opportunity for a man who worked with her. The promotion would bring more responsibility, income, and benefits, but he turned it down. He explained that after considerable prayer, he was convinced that God did not want him to accept the promotion at that time.

My friend pointed out that although this man was sincere and thanked his supervisors for their confidence in him, there would never be another offer. Because he was so bold as to place his future in the hands of God rather than men, he had been blackballed, effectively removed from any future consideration.

The second incident involved a man who had recently become a Christian. Since that event, his entire personality had changed. Not only was he friendlier, but it seemed every sentence was followed by a resounding "Praise God." It didn't matter if he was at his desk, on the phone, in a meeting, or in the elevator. As a result of his "deviant" behavior, he was ostracized by fellow workers. They considered him a clown and made fun of him. Even his work was no longer respected.

My friend was concerned about her own witness. Was she doing the right things? Should she tell her supervisors that she also prayed for guidance? Did God want her to be as overt in her Christianity as her "Praise God" buddy? Her real question was simply, "What does God want me to do as a witness of Him where I work?"

The answer is easy and difficult, simple and complicated. It's easy and simple because the guidelines are already set for us. It can be difficult and complicated because we seek a constant answer where none exists. It is ever-changing. Only its source is constant.

First of all, we know that we must be a Christian for this to have any meaning. We also know that obedience to God has to take priority. We show our love for Him by doing what He tells us to do. You see, that was easy enough. The difficulty lies partly in knowing *what* to do. Here again the guideline is simple.

Our relationship with God is on an individual basis. He sets standards for all of us, but the relationship is unique for each person. What God tells one won't always be what He tells another. Not that there will be contradiction, but each person has a different task in the body of Christ. As the apostle Paul said, some are called to be preachers, some to be teachers, others to be healers and encouragers, and even some to be administrators. There are many different positions in the body of Christ and a number of spiritual gifts, so we shouldn't assume that God will treat us all in the same way.

Likewise, God has called us to do different things in our witness to the world. This is true whether the world is your grocery store, the playground, or where you work.

The real question is, "What does God want *me* to do?"

We can't compare our own walk with that of others as though we should act the same way or say the same things. In my friend's case, she may not have shared the importance she placed on prayer or verbally praised God every few minutes, but does that mean she was failing in her Christian witness? Of course not.

What matters is that we earnestly seek God's will and, when He reveals it, act on it. When we do this, we'll have the confidence of knowing we are doing what God wants in His witness to the world. We should never become burdened with guilt borne from comparing ourselves with others. To do so keeps our minds in the earthly realm and not on the Father. "Set your minds on things above, not on earthly things" (Col. 3:2).

When we fail to focus on God, our witness is ineffective.

We should also be careful not to judge the actions of others. It would have been easy for my friend to decide that these men were wrong, basing her decision on a number of reasons, some even Christian related. But what is the important question here? Were these men doing what they believed God wanted for their individual witness at work? Could it be that God wanted them to have a particular effect in the life of another person?

Let's assume they were following God's directions. Then their actions were demonstrations of love for Him because they obeyed His commands, *and they did so without regard for their status or standing at work.* They put God first. Following His will was the priority in their lives.

Finally, we shouldn't become mired in our own assumptions. Sometimes we fail to let others know we are Christian because of how we view the future. We're afraid opportunities will be lost forever or that we may suffer a drastic setback. We may even try to justify our actions by thinking of all the great things we could do for God later on. It's like trying to bargain with Him. "If we could just forget I'm a Christian for a little while, one day I'll really be able to witness for You."

The bottom line is that we have to remember who God is. He alone issues the commands and sets the standards. Regardless of the situation, if He wants someone to be the president of a company or get a promotion, that will happen—according to His timetable. If we don't believe this, we don't believe He is the Almighty God.

The nature of our witness is in obedience. Dedicate yourself to seeking His will in every situation and to obeying His instructions and commands. We know that we can place our faith and trust in the assurance that God is in control.

⸎

NINETEEN

Seize the Opportunities

Having an effective Christian witness in the business world often requires a new attitude. In our society, we've become a lazy people. So many things are provided for us that we take them for granted and expect them always to be there. We move to the country to get away from urban congestion, yet demand shopping centers and fast food restaurants. A cable TV company sets up shop, and within a few months, everyone demands access to its service.

We become dependent, no longer doing for ourselves, but wanting others to do for us. Many parents don't discipline their children or teach them moral values, choosing to pass off their responsibilities to public schools. Even in our churches, we often fail to witness to others, expecting the paid ministers to carry out what is God's call for each of us. This mind-set becomes a pervasive attitude, affecting everything we think, say, and do.

A Change in Attitude

As Christians, it's important for us to break this attitude. We can no longer wait for someone else to provide the witness we should be giving. We can't *expect* God to deliver to our doorstep wandering souls asking for the way to salvation. We need to look outward, change our way of thinking, and adopt a new approach.

In his letter to the Colossians, Paul confronted a similar problem. Colossae was a commercial city greatly influenced by a mixture of ideas, doctrines, and philosophies. Following this culture, these early Christians blended Jewish ritualism, Oriental mysticism, and Greek philosophy in forming their religious attitudes. The result was a church becoming more interested in tradition, secret knowledge, and human wisdom than the witness it was to give to the lost.

Warning the Colossians not to be deceived by "fine-sounding arguments" (Col. 2:4), Paul urged them to focus on Christ and seek to do His will. Like many of us, they needed a change in attitude, and Paul showed them how to do it. "Devote yourselves to prayer, being watchful and thankful. . . . Be wise in the way you act toward outsiders; make the most of every opportunity" (Col. 4:2, 5).

How to Make a Difference

First, be devoted to prayer. Devotion to prayer means being committed to having fellowship and communication with God. Like the Colossians, we tend to rely on our own ideas and desires. Through prayer, we can better seek and understand God's will and direction. Our focus changes from developing our own plan to listening as God describes His.

Also notice that this devotion should be a continuing state of mind. Paul tells us that regardless of where we are, we should commit to being in constant fellowship with God. It doesn't end when we leave our church or home. We carry this attitude of prayer with us always.

Second, be watchful and thankful. Paul cautions us to be alert to what's going on around us. Pay attention. See with eyes of understanding. Why is this important? What are we to be watchful and alert for? Now this is where the change in attitude really begins.

We are to be watchful and thankful for *opportunities*. These are the special moments God provides so that we may show a witness of Him. God gives the opportunity. He moves people and circumstances to a given point and works on the hearts of men and women to be receptive to His Word.

Do you understand the importance of breaking from the world's mind-set? We can't sit back and expect the witness to be provided for us. We must become those witnesses. We're not just the recipients of good things, but the *messengers* of great tidings. Opportunities arise for others to see Christ in *our* lives, and if we don't respond and allow another to share in our experience of God, they won't see Him!

Third, make the most of every opportunity. God doesn't want us to meet Him halfway. That may be an excellent tactic in negotiations, but it doesn't work here. We can't negotiate with God. We have nothing to offer that He would even remotely be interested in—except every part of our lives and all of our love. Anything less is unacceptable.

When we give a halfhearted effort, we provide a witness that shows exactly how much we love Him. Can you love someone halfway? No. Love is one of those "all-or-nothing" kind of things. We either love God with all our heart, soul, and mind—or we don't love Him at all.

Through Paul, God tells us to wholeheartedly seize every opportunity to witness to others. We may be at home or work, talking with a church member or our boss. We may be with others who can share in the witness or we may be alone. Consider the moment precious, for it has been given by God especially for *your* involvement in His great work.

Finally, be wise in how you act toward others. God knows the best way to witness to each person. There's no set formula to be used in all cases. Sometimes the direct approach is best, while at other times it's more important that someone know how you respond to a given situation and where you place your confidence.

Christ is the wisdom of God (see 1 Cor. 1:24), and if we need wisdom and ask God for it, we know that we'll have it (see James 1:5). "Being wise" in our witness simply means having Christ in our lives. We need to follow Him and not our own desires, for we are God's representatives, and through us, others can see His love. "Be very careful, then, how you live—not as unwise but as wise, making the most of every opportunity, because the days are evil. Therefore do not be foolish, but understand what the Lord's will is" (Eph. 5:15–17).

Strength beyond Fear

In the business world, many Christians fail to witness because of one overriding factor: fear. They're afraid of what others may think, of what may happen to their careers, or of being shunned and ridiculed. But there's another fear I frequently see in many Christians—the fear of failure. It's most often expressed in these terms: "I'm afraid I'll say or do the wrong thing. I just don't want to confuse someone any more than they are. There's so much I don't know, I couldn't possibly help."

These statements have been made by some of the most sincere Christians I've ever known. They love God and want to serve Him, and they understand the importance of leading another to a relationship with God, but they are so afraid of making a mistake that they become paralyzed. Instead of reaching out, they hold back and walk away. Iron-ically, their fear of failure only shows that they have already failed.

The problem lies in the focus of their attention. Each and every statement mentioned above centers on the word *I*. They fail because they don't focus on God. "'No one can come to me unless the Father who sent me draws him'" (John 6:44a).

We don't make another person come to Christ. It doesn't depend on the words we choose or the way we deliver them. We have the command to witness, but it's God who draws them to Himself. No one has ever been saved by a man, woman, or child, but only by the grace of God.

The key is being in fellowship with Him and seeking His will. Know who God is and who you are. As His strength enters us, we don't have to be afraid of saying or doing the wrong thing. Remember His promise! "'But the Counselor, the Holy Spirit, whom the Father will send in my name, will teach you all things and will remind you of ev-erything I have said to you'" (John 14:26).

Jesus has promised that we'll never be alone. He has given us the great Counselor who will teach us everything we need to know and re-mind us of what Jesus has said.

What more could we possibly want? When the opportunity to wit-ness comes, God, through His Holy Spirit, is going to handle every-thing. We don't have to worry about forgetting some Scripture or special point. He'll remind us of what we need to know and do. When we look to Him, He will even tell us what to say.

The effectiveness of the witness doesn't depend on us! Through our obedi-ence, others see a true and faithful witness of God, because He is in con-trol. Through this witness, they not only share a time with us, they have an encounter with God Himself!

The business world is a vast mission field where many need to hear the Word of God. Just as we must take a stand in our homes, we must also take a stand where we work. Whenever we have an oppor-tunity to be involved in God's work, we should make the most of His invitation, being wise in how we act and always focused on His will. In God's peace, we won't be afraid to let others know who we are and Whom we represent. "'Peace I leave with you; my peace I give you. I do not give to you as the world gives. Do not let your hearts be trou-bled and do not be afraid'" (John 14:27).

VI

The Witness
In Church

The God who made the world and everything in it is the Lord of heaven and earth and does not live in temples built by hands.

Acts 17:24

⸎

The Unholy Body

Another transformation in the life of a casual Christian is the *Pious Period* in which he sheds the trappings of home and work to enter a new arena, changing once again as he crosses the threshold of the church. But what is the *church?* I asked a number of churchgoers and here are some typical answers:

> "My church is a wonderful place. We have a large sanctuary that can seat 2,000 people, and a beautiful new family activities center where we can have basketball games and dinners."

> "Well, our church is okay, but we don't have very many members."

> "We're a small church. Our budget isn't very big so we can't do much. But everybody seems to get along."

> "Mine is really a big church. Everybody's heard of it. We even have our own TV show."

> "We're a small country church, only a couple of buildings, but we have a good program for the kids. And those senior adults. Why, they're all the time getting together and going on trips."

The responses usually focused on the number of buildings, programs offered, or members, sometimes including the size of their budget. If a ministry was mentioned, the focus was still on the number of people and activities.

Not one time did anyone describe their church in terms of the godly people who served there. No one ever referred to a fellowship of believers who worship God, are growing in their spiritual walk, and provide an effective example of Christ to the world.

Although we teach that the church is the body of Christ made up of individual Christians working together for the glory of God and His kingdom, we often cling to the external, the material, and what can only be seen on the outside. We may even take pride in this façade, forgetting what's inside.

When the world attacks Christianity, the attack is most often directed against the organization and not the individuals. It's easier to mock an institution with claims of hypocrisy and greed than an old woman on her knees, praying before God. The casual Christian makes this even easier as he takes attitudes from his home and work and applies them to his church. The façade of Christianity becomes the basis for his actions there as well.

In his eyes, the church is just another business that often becomes the object of his adoration. His "church" is only a building program instead of men and women gathering to worship God . . . a television program interested only in ratings and entertainment instead of a hands-on ministry of love in the community . . . a collection of activities to satisfy the demands of its customers instead of a retreat to learn about Christ and how to share Him with the world.

In our discussion of the church, I'm not talking about the organization, the pastor and staff, or the building. The church is the congregation, those individuals who have the responsibility of being the body of Christ. This is important to remember as we look at how the church affects the Christian witness.

The Absence of Leadership

The area in which the casual Christian has been most harmful is church leadership. *His participation alone will destroy much of a congregation's witness to the world!*

Notice that we're not talking about size. Often the influence of the casual Christian will actually increase church membership. Yet nowhere does God tell us that the validity of our witness relates to such numbers. Just because a church has ten thousand members doesn't mean that worship and spiritual growth are occurring there.

Notice that I said *destroy*. The effect of a casual Christian on church leadership is not simply to hinder or delay. His attitudes infect everything, spreading like a disease if not confronted and rebuked, which seldom occurs.

We live in a time when a failure in leadership is immediately brought to our attention. Newspaper headlines and TV reports instantly tell us when a trusted leader has fallen. A president tries to cover up illegal activities. Congressmen and women are caught in a scam. Business executives use confidential information for personal gain. Bank officers authorize bad loans, sending an entire industry into chaos.

The Christian community is certainly not immune. In recent years the specter of fallen leadership has been found in its hallowed halls as well. From televangelists to country preachers. From the church elder to the church secretary. Without leadership, congregations fail to grow spiritually and to become the example of Christ.

The reports on the six o'clock news cause us to doubt and question. A trusted preacher occasionally dipped into church funds until he had stolen a considerable amount of money. He was later convicted and sent to jail. Another attempted to murder his wife . . . to hide evidence that he had killed his first wife! Scams, adultery, prostitution . . . the list is long.

Nonetheless, this isn't where the casual Christian is most effective in destroying the leadership of a church. We have a bad habit of focusing on the fantastic, usually a single rare event, while ignoring the routine, which can affect us much more in the long run.

We usually think only of the pastor, ministerial staff, deacons, and elders as the leaders of the church. Just as important are teachers, choir leaders, and committee members. All are a part of the leadership and each has an effect on the congregation. When there's a lack of leadership, the entire body is affected, not just a portion of it.

"For lack of guidance a nation falls" (Prov. 11:14). This is also true for a congregation. Without leadership, there's no guidance.

Why do casual Christians have such a strong effect here? For many, the answer is a matter of priority. They simply don't see church as an important part of their lives. As a result, they don't provide time to be a part of God's leadership and will use home and work as convenient excuses for their lack of commitment. For example, "I can't do this because [1] I just have too much work or [2] I need to spend time with my kids."

These excuses sound logical on the surface until we realize that his absence is not the exception, but the rule.

The shallowness of these excuses becomes apparent when we look at the rest of the week. The casual Christian has no problem dropping everything and putting work or family aside when there's something else he'd rather do, such as watching television, working on a project, or shooting the breeze with some friends. It's just a question of priority.

His absences and lack of commitment set an example for others to follow. *And others do follow!* The young Christian will learn and adopt the ways and attitudes of those he believes to be living the Christian life. As a result, we see another generation of casual Christians being raised without instruction or guidance, and still others eventually dropping out because of the hypocrisy they see and the frustration they carry. The future of the congregation lies in serious jeopardy.

Business in the Church

Yet the effect of casual Christians goes much deeper. Many of these people *do* come to church, attend committee meetings, discuss issues, and join in the decision making. So, if they are present and participate, what's the problem? Isn't it better to have someone there?

No! Absolutely not! The purpose of Christian leadership is to guide God's people in confronting and resolving spiritual issues in a spiritual manner in the presence of a spiritual God, leading them in spiritual growth as they draw closer to the example of Christ.

Unfortunately, a casual Christian often comes with a poor source of reference, such as the business world. He takes the methods he has learned there and tries to use them in a setting which is foreign and unworkable. Like forcing a square peg into a round hole, they just won't fit.

A few years ago, a small congregation was having a difficult time financially. Programs had to be canceled and plans altered. The finance committee, very concerned about their ability to meet future obligations, met weekly. In one emotional discussion, a man raised his hand to speak.

"You know, it's true the treasury's getting low and we need to be prepared, but I think we need to have more faith in God. This is His church and we're His people. If He wants us to continue, we will. I just think our emphasis should be on prayer and seeking His will."

The chairman looked around in disgust. "We've been talking about this for weeks now and I don't think anyone is really listening. Faith is fine, but it still comes down to how much money you've got in the bank."

In one swift measure, this chairman totally discounted faith in God, gave no credence to the power of prayer, and set a dangerous example for his committee to follow. He was a leader of his church, yet instead of responding in a spiritual manner, he applied the methods of the business world. To him, the future of the church depended not on the will of God, but on a ledger sheet.

In another congregation, the preacher was concerned about their future direction. To get support for *his* plans, he took a businesslike approach, influencing the selection of deacons by opposing certain nominations and pushing others. This caused anger and division which lasted for many years.

The politics and practices of the business world have invaded the sanctity of the church, *and we've come to accept the situation!* We pass it off, saying, "You'll always have that. It's just the way things are, and you have to learn to work with it."

This is nonsense! The body of Christ shouldn't blindly assume such guidelines for how it should act. In *all* things we are to glorify God, even in the way we work together. Yet we often do just the opposite. People are appointed to committees solely on the basis of their careers. Others are selected because they're friendly or popular. Even worse is the appointment that comes only because the position "had to be filled" and some poor soul said yes.

The problem with this decision-making is that it ignores someone very important—God. We fail to consider His will or the spiritual gifts He's given. Once again, we adopt the ways of the world in handling the affairs of an unworldly body. Instead of looking to God, we rely on our own logic. But this doesn't work. In everything we should follow God's will, *even when we don't understand it!*

Once I was involved in the selection of a committee chairman. After much discussion and prayer, a man was chosen. I was horrified. Never in my wildest dreams could I see him with such responsibility. He seldom went to church (I *thought*) and he wasn't very friendly (I *assumed*). It just didn't make sense.

Contrary to my wisdom, he was very capable and did an excellent job. He established his committee on a spiritual basis and sincerely sought God's direction in everything the committee considered. In short, I was wrong.

Now the moral of this story is not that each of us can make a mistake. The purpose is to show that, without thinking, I had adopted a business attitude in how I approached this Christian matter. I didn't go to this man and express my concerns or ask him about his spiritual growth. I made my decision simply on secondary input that had nothing to do with where he stood as a Christian.

The casual Christian often clings to the ways of the business world. Why? First of all, because it's what he is usually most familiar with. Remember, he hides behind a façade of Christianity and doesn't really understand what it means to be a Christian. "The man without the Spirit does not accept the things that come from the Spirit of God, for they are foolishness to him, and he cannot understand them, because they are spiritually discerned" (1 Cor. 2:14).

Prayer before every decision. Counsel from many godly advisors. Seeking God's will rather than reaching for personal desires. Operating on the basis of being sure of what we hope for and certain of what we do not see.

These are ways a congregation should act, but to the casual Christian, they are foolishness. "It may have been fine in Jesus' day, but things are different now. We have more information and can make better decisions."

Faith above a ledger? Welcoming a different race or culture with little money to support the church while knowing that such action will send the big tithers away? Taking a public stand based on Christian conviction that's not popular in the community?

The casual Christian can't understand because he's a part of the world. When we put him in a position of leadership, he responds according to the expectations of this world. God is forgotten. "His will be done" becomes only a monotonous refrain.

And the congregation falls for lack of godly guidance.

⌒◯⌒

The Sinking Fellowship

The casual Christian also has a devastating effect within the fellowship of a congregation. Here again he takes from what he knows best and tries to make it fit within the walls of the church.

Image is everything. Remember the commercial? This is true not only for the casual Christian as he works and plays, but in his church life as well. It isn't enough to belong to a fellowship. He wants that fellowship to have the image of success.

But what is success?

In the world's view, a business is a success when it makes it to the top and is regarded as number one. It may be the largest or the wealthiest. It may control a market or an entire industry. All in all, it carries the image of success and there's no mistaking it.

The casual Christian brings this attitude to his church and applies the same criteria. Sadly, many of us, with good intentions, join in this comparison game and fall into the trap without a thought in the world.

What church would you consider very successful? We usually point to the mega-church and look in awe at the huge size of its membership or budget. It has a large TV audience, a youth program for hundreds of children, and a singles ministry with social activities twice a week. Its calendars are filled with events for all ages, and its choirs tour the country.

Using the world's standards, we focus on the surface, getting lost in its elaborate Christmas cantata or how many softball teams it has. But we lose sight of something more important: its spiritual responsibilities. Is the church reaching its community for Christ? Is it leading Christians into a deeper relationship with God or training them to minister to the lost, the needy, the sick, and the lonely?

Real success is reaching people for Christ and helping them grow closer to God. Nothing more, nothing less. It doesn't depend on numbers, not even the number of baptisms. If a person doesn't understand what he's doing in committing his life to Christ, the numbers are meaningless.

Yet everywhere we turn, special recognition is given to the greatest and the grandest. The basis for such recognition? Numbers. The reason? The casual Christian has entrenched within the Christian community the desire to compare and compete. We don't applaud a congregation simply for a good effort or job well done. We honor it because it has the highest numbers.

If there is any acknowledgment at all, shouldn't it be for doing God's will? If so, it would seem that comparison and competition serve no useful purpose. Comparison alone can serve to educate, but when used for competition, it can bolster the pride of a few and leave others discouraged.

Out of Sight, Out of Mind

The casual Christian's drive for success has major side effects. Two especially cause severe harm to our witness.

Under the casual Christian's leadership and influence, the image of the church becomes very important. Slogans are created and programs chosen based upon the promotion of this image. The name of a church may even be changed to appease a potentially critical public. Some churches remove steeples and crosses from their buildings so that visitors may feel more comfortable as they come to hear motivational speeches on self-worth that have replaced sermons on the grace of God.

But such drastic measures don't have to occur for congregations to feel the deep effects of the casual Christian. He's guided us to focus on the surface, ignoring what's inside, and this is reflected in how we act toward each other.

When we go to a church service, we often hear of people in need of prayer. Some are sick and dying. Others are hurting financially. A few express concern for relatives and friends who don't know Christ. We often respond, "Oh, yes. I'll remember you in my prayers." The words come like a reflex, but we fail to keep our promise. Following the casual Christian, we can easily project only an image of caring and concern. The façade of Christianity spreads.

Some time ago I counseled a man who was deeply depressed. He had been sick for several weeks and had fallen behind in his work. When he returned to his job, he had to go out of town for an extended period.

Part of his depression was caused by loneliness and a sense of rejection. He was a regular churchgoer and enjoyed the fellowship. But because of his illness and work, he hadn't been there for eight weeks. During that time, no one called, wrote a note, or came to visit. Deep down he was fighting a conclusion he'd already accepted—his church really didn't care.

Focusing on the surface, the numbers, and the image, the casual Christian loses sight of the value of that one individual. He leads his congregation in a great display of glory to the Lord, but fails to care for His sheep. This is especially obvious among the sick and elderly who can no longer come to church or to many church functions. We give them the status of "shut-ins" and often forget about them.

This lack of caring is also shown in another interesting way. Remember that in everything, the casual Christian seeks his own satisfaction, including his choice of churches. This is no more evident than when he decides it is time for a change.

Over the years I've heard many reasons for leaving a church: disapproval of a church decision, bad preaching, depressing church services, a changing community, a problem with another church member, and so forth. Sound familiar?

For the casual Christian, these are logical reasons. After all, he makes decisions every day based on his likes and dislikes. But notice the center of attention here. Once again, it's his own satisfaction he is seeking.

A common reason given for leaving a church is, "It's for the good of the children." Usually, the parent has been comparing and found what he considers to be a *successful* youth ministry. "They must have three times the number of kids in their program, and every year they go to the beach in the summer and on a ski trip in the winter."

What's wrong here? The emphasis is on numbers and activities, not the ability of a youth ministry to lead children to Christ and guide them in spiritual growth. In all the years I worked with youth, I was seldom told that a family left for a church that better met the children's spiritual needs. I was never told a family actually spent the effort to determine if another youth ministry could better meet such needs. More often than not, parents either use their children as an excuse to hide their true reasons for leaving or try to make themselves feel better by giving them an image of what appears to be good. Either way, they're seeking their own satisfaction.

The problem is that we've forgotten something basic about each congregation. Regardless of its denomination or size, every body of believers has its own mission. Certainly we are all in the effort to witness to the world, but how this is accomplished remains an individual matter determined by God for that local church.

Some congregations have become centers to help those with alcohol dependencies. While their doors are open to all, their mission lies with alcoholics and their families. Others provide food, clothing, and shelter to the homeless, counseling for the troubled, and assistance to the disabled. Some provide adoption services, placing children in Christian homes, and operate pregnancy crisis centers, counseling unwed mothers.

But because he is self-centered, the casual Christian never adopts the mission. He claims to be a member, but is never a part of what the congregation is doing. Other than giving some lip service and money every now and then, he's simply along for the ride.

With this attitude, he sees a church in terms of what he can get out of it. The worship service is just a time when he can be entertained. This attitude is passed along to his children who complain about boring Bible lessons. They want to go on youth trips to the beach, the mountains, or amusement parks, but not to meetings to get closer to God.

So he leaves for that new place where he can be catered to and satisfied, never taking the time to find out if God wants him to leave. After all, that would take away *his* control of *his* life and might not satisfy *his* desires or the needs of *his* image. So he moves, terminating one relationship and beginning a new one, as though he were clocking in and out at work.

Caring, concern, and love have taken a backseat to the casual Christian's compelling desire to satisfy himself. He looks after number one as he seeks his own happiness. Though we should put the interests of others ahead of our own, the casual Christian embraces the teachings of the world and just can't understand.

The Bitter Root

There remains one critical way a casual Christian can affect the life of a church, the attitude of a congregation, and the spiritual growth of its members. The awesome power of this influence can destroy and devastate. Its outburst may last only seconds, but its fury endures for generations. It separates and divides, opening a door for hatred and spite. And it's found when there's conflict.

A few years ago, I gave a seminar on reconciliation and how to resolve disputes among Christians. In my talk I made the point that each time we believe someone has wronged us, regardless of how it occurs, we have the responsibility to try immediately to reconcile with that person.

Afterwards, an old pastor thanked me for sharing with the group, but proceeded to tell me this was one area that required time and experience, and he was certain I would be changing my talk as I got older. When I asked him why he felt that way, he said, "Well, sometimes you just have to let sleeping dogs lie. No matter what you do, it won't help. I once had this minister of education . . . ."

He told me about a staff member who had expressed to a few church members his disapproval of certain actions taken by the pastor. When told of this, the pastor went to the deacons and had him fired. He said he never spoke to him about it because he knew it would do no good. But the truth was that he wanted to avoid confrontation, and his decision violated Jesus' clear instruction: "'If your brother sins against you, go and show him his fault, just between the two of you'" (Matt. 18:15a).

It's very important for us to understand that this is not a suggestion. Jesus never said, "Oh, here's something you might try." *This is a command!*

Yet we ignore it every day. Why? Because it's hard, and it makes us uneasy. It forces us to confront another person, something most of us want to avoid. Instead of facing a situation, we sit back and say "It's not that big a deal" or "Time will heal all wounds."

These statements only mislead and confuse. Until we follow Christ's command, there will be no healing, and the hurt and bitterness will remain. We'll call on that memory at a moment's notice to justify an attitude or emotion about that person.

Jesus warns us to try to resolve the problem immediately: "'Settle matters quickly'" (Matt. 5:25a). Paul also saw the danger: "Do not let the sun go down while you are still angry, and do not give the devil a foothold" (Eph. 4:26b–27).

While it's true that the casual Christian has a profound effect here, what's even more troubling is the careless way so many of us blindly follow in his footsteps. When we choose not to reconcile with a brother, our anger festers over time, growing until it affects everything about us—our reactions to others, our views of life, and our love for one another. We become bitter souls and isolate ourselves from the one we believe caused all the trouble, refusing to speak or acknowledge his presence.

This anger can destroy a person's life. If kept inside, it can harm his mental and physical health. But there remains an even greater result of this disobedience. "'As I have loved you, so you must love one another. All men will know that you are my disciples, if you love one another'" (John 13:34b–35). If we're to be the light of the world and let others see Christ in our lives, they should see something very different from what's in the world. Jesus told us what that something is: the way we act toward other Christians.

When the world takes a long look at us, it should see people who truly love each other. If there are disputes or wrongs, the world should see Christians rushing to resolve the problem and reconcile their relationship. The *relationship* among Christians is of the utmost importance, always greater than who may be right or wrong. Why? Because we're to love each other, and this unique love is a powerful witness to the world that we follow Jesus.

Does this describe you and your congregation? If it does, then praise the Lord! You are unique indeed. But if not, then there's serious work to be done.

The Believers

And he will go before the Lord, in the spirit and power of Elijah, to turn the
hearts of the fathers to their children and the disobedient to the wisdom of the
righteous—to make ready a people prepared for the Lord.

Luke 1:17

As we look at the Christian witness today, it's important to remember, first of all, that the confusion caused by the casual Christian is not the result of a conscious decision to undermine Christianity. It's the determined work of another author—Satan. "But if you harbor bitter envy and selfish ambition in your hearts, do not boast about it or deny the truth. Such 'wisdom' does not come down from heaven but is earthly, unspiritual, of the devil" (James 3:14–15).

Secondly, we're not the ones actually tackling this problem. The battle belongs to Jesus, and His power is greater than anything we'll ever encounter. "'All authority in heaven and on earth has been given to me. . . . And surely I am with you always, to the very end of the age'" (Matt. 28:18, 20). "The one who is in you is greater than the one who is in the world" (1 John 4:4b).

The power of God is present in our lives, but we often forget about it. We cower in fear and fail to bear the witness we have a responsibility to share. We fail because we're not prepared.

I chose the opening passage for this chapter because in its references to John the Baptist, this verse also describes the function of the most important area of Christian life: the church. It may sound strange to give it such importance. For some, it's just a place to gather once or twice a week to meet friends and maybe learn a little about God. Many would give greater emphasis to the home and family. Yet while I don't want to lessen the importance of our work there, the church takes priority.

In this special fellowship, we can learn how to live like a Christian, regardless of where we may be. How we raise our children, treat one another, or handle situations at work should all be based on lessons learned in God's place of instruction. Through such teaching, the church provides one of its greatest functions: making ready a people prepared for the Lord.

Sometimes we hear that the church should be a "place of worship," but that phrase is easily spoken and seldom understood. If the church doesn't teach its people, how can they know what worship is or even how to worship? The body of Christians should also provide the spiritual growth Christ has ordained since the beginning of time. The basics of the Christian church can be found in the Book of Acts.

First We Wait

"'Do not leave Jerusalem, but wait for the gift my Father promised. . . . You will receive power when the Holy Spirit comes on you; and you will be my witnesses in Jerusalem, and in all Judea and Samaria, and to the ends of the earth'" (Acts 1:4b, 8a). This message has been the subject of countless sermons, Bible studies, and Sunday School lessons. It gives hope, confidence, and faith. The instruction we hear is to spread the gospel of Jesus Christ throughout the world. But if we only glance at the surface of the words, we miss deeper instructions which are critical to God's people and the witness of the individual.

Jesus' first instruction is: *Wait!*

The disciples were undoubtedly excited at this time. Their Lord, whom they thought was lost to the grave, had returned. He stayed many days, teaching and allowing their understanding of God's will to grow. They grew bolder and, I'm sure, were very eager to get started in this work. But Jesus told them, "Wait! Don't leave Jerusalem. You're not prepared for the ministry yet."

Even when the work was to begin, Jesus gave them a carefully laid out plan. "First be my witnesses in Jerusalem. Then look to Judea and Samaria. Finally, go throughout the world." This isn't simply Jesus telling them to spread the gospel. These are His instructions for how to do it. By understanding them, we'll see how He wants His people to function today and why, even with the best of intentions, we so often fail.

"Wait! Don't leave Jerusalem. Don't get excited and try to spread my message just yet. It's too soon!" The emphasis here is on being prepared. Although these men had been with Jesus for several years, they still weren't ready.

These words of caution are just as important to us as they were to the disciples. Before we can be witnesses for Christ, we must first be prepared. When each of us becomes a Christian, we have the gift of the Holy Spirit, but we often lock Him away and don't receive His power. Why? Because we haven't grown spiritually. Remember, we are newborns in the family of God, and there's a lot for us to learn.

Preparation Begins with Caring

One problem in many churches is not recognizing that new Christians know very little and have a desperate need to grow spiritually. Far too often, men, women, and children claim Jesus as their Lord and Savior, only to find that their mountaintop experience doesn't last. They return home, go to their jobs, seek out old haunts, and nothing has changed.

Sometimes it's because there wasn't a conversion to begin with. The person reacts out of emotion and not on personal conviction. But he'll also return to "old habits" when no effort is made to welcome this child of God and make him ready for the Lord's service. This needs to start from the very beginning.

Something I've seen in many churches has always struck me as very sad. I'm a Southern Baptist, and at the close of a typical Baptist service, an invitation is given for anyone to say publicly that he's become a Christian. A man will nervously walk down the aisle to the pastor, who warmly greets him. After the congregation is told the good news that he's accepted Christ as Lord and Savior, they are encouraged to come down and welcome him.

I find this sad for two reasons. First, it often lacks celebration. I'm certain that when a poor soul accepts the calling of the Holy Spirit, there's a tremendous shout in heaven. Bells ring, angels sing. There are laughter, smiles, and deep joy. The cheering must be deafening. Our heavenly Father beams with eternal love.

Meanwhile, back at the ranch, very little is happening. Oh, maybe a few tears and some smiles, but no resounding "Amens!" or "Praise God!" or even an enthusiastic "All right!" Shouldn't this at least equal a last ditch touchdown pass that wins the Super Bowl or a grand slam home run that wins the World Series? It should not only be equal but go light-years beyond!

A soul has been spared the eternal pain and suffering of a horrible hell—all through the grace of a loving Father. Another person has been added to the family of God, and yet we sit and nod some faint approval. Christians should be echoing Paul's words, "Rejoice in the Lord always. I will say it again: Rejoice!" (Phil. 4:4).

The second reason is similar to the first, though it tells more of who we really are and points to our own spiritual shallowness. The pastor says a sweet benediction, the choir sings softly, and the service comes to a close. The new convert stands before God's people, still nervous but also excited about meeting his new family and friends. Then he watches as most of them stand, turn their backs, and walk away. They never even glance in his direction, let alone come to welcome him into this *marvelous* family.

This isn't unique to Baptist churches. In my travels, I've seen the same rejection acted out in many denominations. Just as Peter denied his Lord, we, in this way, deny His love and kindness to our new brother or sister. There's nothing like the joy of genuine acceptance or the warmth provided by people who really care. (And dear friends, this is nothing like it!) Preparation begins with caring, and it should begin as soon as we enter the family of God.

Accepting Someone's Gifts

Jesus told the disciples to be patient. Yes, it was important to spread the Word, but before they could begin the work even in their own backyard, they had to wait; wait for the gift of God to come into in their lives; wait for the Holy Spirit; and wait to be made ready for His service.

Of course, we really hate waiting. Through peer pressure, incessant pleading, or endless guilt, we urge new members to become *involved*. This may be teaching, directing, witnessing, chaperoning, or serving on committees, but we seldom take the time to make them ready. In other words, we send them out into Jerusalem before they've learned how to use the spiritual gifts God has given them. Simply put, we fail to follow Christ's instructions to the first church.

In our eagerness to encourage participation, we sometimes make matters worse by forcing them into positions we don't know they can handle. Even with the best of intentions, frustration, guilt, and anger can easily result. We become masters of discouragement, unknowingly setting the stage for burnout and increased absences.

Before we can run, we must learn to walk. Before we walk, we must crawl. And before we crawl, we must totally depend on someone else.

Before a Christian is ready, useful for the Master, and prepared to do any good work, he is totally dependent on Jesus, who re-forms him through the Holy Spirit and through us. This new Christian has yet to crawl. For his sake and the work of the kingdom, we shouldn't force him to run until he has first learned the basic steps. Even then, we should be careful to encourage and not direct, for only God knows the path set before each person. We are wrong when we pressure others into jobs God never intended them to have.

A friend of mine is a dear, wonderful person. She has good insight, a loving heart, and a humbleness that shines as an example for others. But she's not the outgoing kind who can walk up to a stranger and start talking. Because her church requires all church leaders to visit new members, she declines many positions she could easily handle.

Visitation makes her very uncomfortable and serves as a constant burden. Instead of encouragement in the use of her spiritual gifts, she's told she must be involved in everything, not just her special job within the body of Christ. The result? Frustration, deep guilt, and more refusals to accept leadership positions because she doesn't feel worthy. Discouragement reigns.

This isn't what Christ intended! He wants each of us to serve Him in the way *He* has chosen, and the church should help His people get ready for these tasks.

How? We can help each other discover our spiritual gifts. We can suggest areas of Christian work that need these special abilities and learn how to use them. Above all, we can pray and share with one another as encouragement to ask God for direction, seek His will, and knock at the door of opportunity He provides.

⌒∞⌒

Preparation

How do God's people prepare themselves for His work? The first church gives us the answer: "They devoted themselves to the apostles' teaching and to the fellowship, to the breaking of bread and to prayer" (Acts 2:42).

The focus here is in four areas: (1) the apostles' teaching—the study of God's Word, (2) the fellowship—encouragement among believers, (3) the breaking of bread—the Lord's Supper, and (4) prayer. Without a solid foundation in each of these areas, a Christian isn't ready for God's service. In spite of good intentions, what he tries to do for the kingdom will fail and his witness of Christ will suffer.

The Lord's Supper concerns our remembrance of Christ, specifically understanding who God is, what He's done for us in Christ Jesus, and who we are in relation to Him. Since we've already discussed this area, we'll concentrate here on the study of God's Word, prayer, and, in the next chapter, encouragement among believers.

Studying the Word of God

Christians in the first church devoted themselves to the apostles' teaching. They listened to the disciples and learned about God's mercy, love, and grace. They were taught of the Messiah coming as Jesus Christ, who was crucified on the cross but raised in triumph over death. And most importantly, they learned that they could be saved and reconciled to the Father.

We've already seen that when we don't study God's Word, we can't understand who He is and, consequently, who we are in relation to

Him. This understanding is essential if we are to live as Christ commanded.

It's also important that this be done within a congregation, where the knowledge gained by sharing with others can often be many times more than what we get on our own. As God speaks to His people, He lays a different degree of insight on each person's heart. In the fellowship of other Christians, we have the wonderful opportunity to learn from another's understanding and experiences. The old saying, "The only way to learn something is by doing it yourself," just isn't true for spiritual knowledge.

When it comes to spiritual growth, however, we can be a very stubborn people, not taking another's word for anything—not even God's Word. And though He warns that there's no life under the sun, that happiness can't be found in money, power, or sex, many run off to find out for themselves.

Jesus knew this about human nature. In the parable of the prodigal son, He told of a child who had everything he needed but wanted more. Against his father's wishes, he went out into the world, only to lose everything he had. Finally humbling himself, he came home where his father accepted him back with loving arms.

Like the prodigal son, we often rush out to see the world for ourselves. We make many mistakes, and sometimes our lives lie in ruins. But as children of God, when we head back home, our Father takes us back.

When we study God's Word and listen to His teaching, we learn without the pain and sorrow, without the loss and humiliation. We don't have to be like the prodigal son, at least not over and over again.

Think of the love and faithfulness of God we learn about in this parable, as well as in the life of Jesus, the lives of the apostles, and the prophets. These lessons give us hope and security when the world strikes us down. But how do we know if not by studying His Word? How can we grow spiritually if we're not taught?

The importance of devoutly teaching the Word of God can't be overstated. The effectiveness of our witness in the world desperately depends on it. When we fail to train God's people properly, the church becomes dormant, accomplishing nothing in the spiritual realm.

For a number of years, many churches de-emphasized training new Christians. Failing to see its importance, they confined such instruction to a single program usually held only once a week. Over time, even the program came to have little significance, often giving way to other activities such as dinners and football games.

As a result, an entire generation of church members were raised who believe Christian life is centered around a Sunday morning service. Church leaders may seek to reach out to the lost and the hurting, but this new generation fails to respond. They haven't been taught how to live a life worthy of Christ in every way for every day.

Throughout our churches, across denominations, and in movements such as Promise Keepers and Precept Ministries, a growing number of men and women are willing to take their faith seriously and learn to live as Christians. If you are one of them, the Word of God is your invaluable source of guidance, regardless of how much you've grown spiritually. It's up to all of us to make certain it is being taught.

Prayer

Many churches make an effort to teach something of the Holy Scriptures. Though some have abandoned the Word for the "enlightened" views of modern writers or for a more "progressive" attitude toward heightened awareness of social issues, those, if they still choose to be called Christian, are in the minority. Still, too few concentrate on the second basis of a well-founded church: prayer.

Being devoted to prayer means more than just praying. If we're devoted to an activity, we learn everything we can so that our participation in it will be more effective. The same is true with prayer. When we're devoted, we not only pray more, we also learn what prayer is and how we can pray effectively.

Unfortunately, this is where churches often drop the ball. While encouraging prayer, they fail to teach their members *regularly* what prayer is or how they should pray. There's the occasional sermon or Bible study, but for the most part, Christians are treated as though they should instinctively know and understand. After all, it's just talking to the Big Man Upstairs. Right?

Wrong! Prayer is serious business and shouldn't be taken lightly. Jesus stressed its importance, though many of us often miss the point. While God also speaks to us through His Word, prayer is entirely different. We're not limited to being on the receiving end only, as when we read the Bible. In prayer, we have the opportunity to speak and express our concerns, fears, hurts, and sorrows with Someone who listens.

The First Purpose of Prayer

The first purpose of prayer is the development of an intimate relationship with God. But how is this relationship developed? How do we become intimate with God? Jesus gives the answer by teaching us how to pray: "'Our Father in heaven, hallowed be your name, your kingdom come, your will be done on earth as it is in heaven. Give us today our daily bread. Forgive us our debts, as we also have forgiven our debtors. And lead us not into temptation, but deliver us from the evil one'" (Matt. 6:9–13).

First, acknowledge with whom you're speaking. When we pray, we address a holy God, the same who created all things simply through the sound of His voice.

Several years ago a character in a TV show would occasionally pray, beginning something like this, "Hey, Big Guy Upstairs. It's C. Graham here." The audience would always laugh. In reality, prayer is not a joking matter. God, while merciful and kind, remains awesome and deserving of our utmost respect, honor, and praise. He's not our Big Buddy in the Sky. That attitude may be fine if we're talking to an equal, but with God, we don't even come close.

Second, Jesus says to address God as Father. This is a serious step in developing an intimate relationship. Instead of being reminded that He's the Lord God Almighty, we're to come as His obedient children.

Third, focus your first requests on God and His will. "May You be regarded as holy, may Your kingdom be established now, and may Your will be carried out in this world." Jesus tells us that our primary concern is not our own desires or wants. Instead, we're to ask that God's glory and kingdom be exalted. The effect of this is to clarify our position before God (in other words, to humble us). Prayer not only reminds us who God is, but also who we are in relation to Him. It's our way of echoing what John the Baptist once said about Jesus: "He must become greater; I must become less" (John 3:30).

Next, ask for your daily bread. Like many of Jesus' teachings, this has a double meaning. On the surface, we're told to ask for what is necessary to survive. This is represented by the simplicity of bread. Jesus didn't say to wish for a banquet, but to ask for what we need.

There's a deeper message here as well. We should also pray to be filled with the Holy Spirit and Christ's teachings each and every day. Jesus is the spiritual nourishment we so desperately need. "'I am the bread of life. He who comes to me will never go hungry, and he who believes in me will never be thirsty'" (John 6:35).

As we pray, our focus should first be on God, secondly on the glory of His kingdom and His will, and thirdly on the lordship of Christ in our lives. We claim an intimate relationship with our heavenly Father and we ask only for our essential needs.

In the fourth part of this prayer, Jesus says to look at our relationships with others as we humble ourselves before God. We are to ask forgiveness, but we must be careful not to miss the important condition here. We ask that forgiveness be given to us in the same way that we have forgiven others.

The point is to forgive others. We must be rid of the bitterness and anger that dwell in an unforgiving heart. Jesus set the terms when He told His disciples, "'Love one another. As I have loved you, so you must love one another'" (John 13:34). The command is clear. We should love others in a way that places their needs ahead of our own, a self-sacrificing love demonstrated by action and not mere sentimentality.

Even in our prayers, Jesus wants us to remember our posture before God and man. We are to become servants, and our prayers should be a constant affirmation of our commitment to Christ's commands for our lives.

Finally, Jesus says to pray that we not fall into the hands of Satan and the temptations of the world. Again we are reminded of who we really are. We don't have the strength to fight every temptation but must rely on God's strength if we're to make it through each day. Jesus wants us to be ever-mindful that in this world there is something that is evil and far too great for us to handle alone.

Through this prayer, sincerely offered, we have to be honest with God and ourselves. We see more clearly who He is and, perhaps painfully, who we are. We can't build a façade or hide behind a false image. Through such honesty, the stage is set for frank discussions and the growth of an intimate relationship.

God's people, to carry out Christ's ministry effectively, must teach each other how to pray and, by doing so, develop a real prayer ministry. As we've already seen, before God will draw closer to us, we have to draw closer to Him. Prayer provides the avenue for this to occur.

The Second Purpose of Prayer

The second purpose of prayer is the development of faith. Jesus made several promises when it came to prayer. "'If two of you on earth agree about anything you ask for, it will be done for you by my Father in heaven. For where two or three come together in my name, there am I with them'" (Matt. 18:19–20). "'Therefore I tell you, whatever you ask for in prayer, believe that you have received it, and it will be yours'" (Mark 11:24).

Now Jesus has already taught us how to pray, but look at the confidence He says we should have. "Believe that you have received it, and it will be yours." "If two or more come together in prayer, I am there with you." "Ask and it will be done."

These promises are difficult for many Christians to accept, but not because they don't want to. They just can't believe it's that simple. The church hasn't been the training ground it should be. When a church's ministry is not based on a solid foundation of prayer, its members will seldom have a prayer life of their own. They have no example or encouragement.

In the Book of Acts, the first church took prayer seriously and prayed constantly. Paul urged his readers to "pray in the Spirit on all occasions with all kinds of prayers and requests" (Eph. 6:18a). He realized that consistent prayer, in this manner, would grow them spiritually, develop closer relationships with God, and strengthen their faith as they saw His faithfulness in answering their requests.

"Now faith is being sure of what we hope for and certain of what we do not see" (Heb. 11:1). *Being sure of what we hope for* is the foundation of our prayers. We make our requests relying on the assurance of His promises. *Being certain of what we do not see* is the confidence that our prayers are heard and will be answered.

Paraphrasing the definition in Hebrews, faith is the surrender of the autonomy of the human mind to the will of God. When we pray as Jesus taught, our purest expression of faith is prayer. We give up control and acknowledge God's authority. In prayer we present a clear witness of Christ to a lost world.

When a congregation fails to pray consistently as a body of believers, it's impossible for them to be close to God, seek His guidance, or know His will. Without a firm foundation rooted in prayer, faith has no means of expression and is nothing more than words spoken in the wind.

The body of Christ deserves a better understanding of prayer. Encouraging prayer chains, prayer groups, and prayer partners can demonstrate its effectiveness, and having prayer before all meetings and services can signify its importance. But as in all spiritual matters, care must be taken. Prayer should always be a reflection of a sincere heart and never just a ritual.

cℬ

Encouragement

In preparing for God's work, Christians are called to encourage each other in their spiritual growth. Unfortunately, teaching them how to encourage is given little attention and in many churches is ignored completely.

We often assume that loving and caring for one another will just happen and encouragement will naturally follow, but encouragement is not a natural outgrowth of how we feel toward someone else. As in studying God's Word and in prayer, true, consistent encouragement requires a conscious effort of determined action.

Because of our natural tendencies, most of us lean toward those things which are easy and simple. Encouragement is neither. It's usually hard work, involving a lot of effort over long periods of time. In fact, encouraging another person can be very frustrating and exhausting.

The Role of Encouragement

The importance of encouragement is found throughout the Bible. Noah encouraged his family, and as a result their lives were spared. Aaron was a huge encouragement to Moses in dealing with the Egyptians and with their own people. Through the encouragement of Barnabas, Paul gained acceptance and confidence that aided him in the spread of the gospel throughout the world.

In the New Testament, Paul repeatedly calls us to be encouragers. His pleas for encouragement are clearly stated in his letters to the

Romans, Corinthians, Ephesians, Philippians, Colossians, and Thessalonians, as well as in his letters to Timothy, Titus, and Philemon. The writer of Hebrews also stresses encouragement, as does Peter.

The repetition of a subject is God's indication that it is very important. It therefore becomes equally important for us to understand the full meaning of what He's telling us. When it comes to encouragement, its significance is summed up in a simple passage that, oddly enough, doesn't even mention the word: "Two are better than one, because they have a good return for their work: If one falls down, his friend can help him up. But pity the man who falls and has no one to help him up!" (Eccles. 4:9–10).

As we go through life, each of us needs encouragement, whether we're dealing with the world or struggling with our Christian growth. When the Bible says to pity the man who has no one to help him, we are to understand that encouragement is important in the life of God's people.

What is encouragement? We usually think of it only in terms of an uplifting, even cheerful, prodding toward some worthy goal, but it encompasses much more.

Encouragement is an act of inspiring, guiding, motivating, and stimulating. It isn't teaching in and of itself or the process of instruction, but the atmosphere, presence, or words that are meant to influence an outcome. In this way, we *urge* someone on to a particular goal.

It is this aspect of encouragement that comes to mind most often and usually in positive terms. The Bible frequently refers to encouragement as a part of training, teaching, and strengthening. In Deuteronomy 3:28, God told Moses to encourage Joshua so that he could lead the Israelites into the promised land after his death. Moses was to do everything necessary to train, teach, and instruct Joshua *so that he would be prepared to do God's work.*

Urging someone to achieve higher goals definitely has a positive side, but there is also a tougher aspect of encouragement. It's this other side we seldom see in congregations today. Many Christians may not even understand it to be a part of encouragement, or they may simply choose to ignore it. Yet if God's people are to effectively encourage each other, they should also be ready to rebuke.

Encourage and Rebuke

Paul saw rebuking as a part of the overall ministry of encouragement. "I give you this charge: Preach the Word; be prepared in season and out of season; correct, rebuke and encourage—with great patience and careful instruction" (2 Tim. 4:1–2). "Encourage and rebuke with all authority" (Titus 2:15b).

Rebuking is seldom exercised in the average church today. The very thought of taking such action often brings strong resistance. But if the Bible calls for us to rebuke our brothers and sisters in Christ, why do we resist? There are two primary reasons.

First, we convince ourselves that rebuking is the same as *judging*. We recall Christ warning that when we judge others, that the same measure by which we judge will also be used to judge us. Paul also strongly cautions us against judging others, saying that only God can judge.

The problem with this line of thinking is that rebuking, as described in the Bible, doesn't involve judging at all. When a person judges someone else, he's making his own determination as to what is good or bad, right or wrong. Judging uses an *independent* analysis and conclusion.

Rebuking, however, doesn't depend on what we think. It makes absolutely no difference if we feel something was good or bad. It doesn't depend on our reasoning or logical analysis. Instead, rebuking is merely the application of what God has specifically set down. We're not passing judgment, only stating fact.

For example, today it's not unusual to find men and women involved in extramarital affairs. Almost always, these affairs are strongly defended by shifting blame from the unfaithful spouse. We're told that this pathetic figure is extremely lonely, constantly ignored, and has needs for intimate companionship and affection that aren't being met. This popular argument is the basis for claims of emotional distress, but it is most effective in its diversion from what the act truly is—adultery.

When we look to God's Word for its treatment of extramarital affairs, we're not judging anyone. God has already done that. We're just stating a fact: An extramarital affair is adultery, a violation of God's command, and therefore a wrong thing for a Christian to do.

When we rebuke someone, we're bringing this fact to his attention. We are instructed to do this not for the purpose of condemnation, but to urge him to live a life worthy of Christ as we all have been called to do. Rebuking is a part of encouraging a person in his spiritual growth.

The second reason why many Christians refuse to rebuke someone is that it makes them feel uncomfortable. It may even open the door for them to be rebuked as well. Part of this is well founded. It's never an easy thing to do, but it helps if we focus on the function of rebuking and how to carry it out.

Rebuking is not done to humiliate someone. It's a very important part of helping him develop spiritually. Rebuking can be characterized as discipline, but notice how this kind of discipline is described. "That word of encouragement that addresses you as sons: 'My son, do not make light of the Lord's discipline, and do not lose heart when he rebukes you, because the Lord disciplines those he loves, and he punishes everyone he accepts as a son'" (Heb. 12:5–6).

Rebuking, if done this way, is *always* founded in love. Out of love, we rebuke someone so that he may grow as a Christian, not as a means of tearing him down. How is this accomplished in love? "Love is patient, love is kind. It does not envy, it does not boast, it is not proud. It is not rude, it is not self-seeking, it is not easily angered, it keeps no record of wrongs. Love does not delight in evil but rejoices with the truth. It always protects, always trusts, always hopes, always perseveres. Love never fails" (1 Cor. 13:4–8a).

This is our guideline when we rebuke one another. There's no hatred, anger, or animosity. There's no joy in someone else's failure, nor is there an ongoing account of his errors. We don't rebuke in order to promote *ourselves*.

Instead, we rebuke only out of love and in a way that is patient and kind. We're not rude in our correction but always seek to protect each other as we grow in Christ. Above all, we place the direction of the rebuking in the hands of Jesus who is faithful to guide us in this effort.

Encouragement involves many different actions and attitudes. It's a part of the teaching and instruction God has planned for His children. It's that consistent urging to grow spiritually and live as Christ would have us live. And it's also that stern rebuking we sometimes need to guide us back to God. But in all things and in all ways, encouragement is the result of love.

The first church had the awesome task of preparing early Christians for ministry in the world. So that they would be ready to do His work, Jesus told them to go through a time of preparation founded on studying God's Word, prayer, and encouragement among the believers. He knew that only through such effort, training, and instruction would His people be capable of doing the work He had assigned. God set the procedure and He alone set the timetable.

The church is no different today. Newborn Christians continually present themselves before congregations and must be taught and trained. These *children* must be shown the way that Christ wants us to live. And they must be loved.

There's no better place for this love and encouragement to be shared than in the family of God. His people have this task. If we're to be effective in carrying out the ministry of Christ, we will meet this responsibility. "See to it, brothers, that none of you has a sinful, unbelieving heart that turns away from the living God. But encourage one another daily, as long as it is called Today, so that none of you may be hardened by sin's deceitfulness" (Heb. 3:12–13).

VII

The Witness
In Our Community

I tell you the truth,
whatever you did for one of the least of these brothers of mine,
you did for me.

Matthew 25:40

The Abandoned Community

William Shakespeare once wrote that the world is a stage on which people enter, act out their parts, and exit. This is true. As we come into this life, mature, grow old, and depart, we take on many roles: child, teenager, young adult, employee, employer, student, teacher, parent, friend, and confidant. We move from one to another, assuming different responsibilities, expectations, goals, and desires. These roles play a significant part in defining who we are.

And this is how it should be. Each life undergoes change. We move, develop, and adjust. But if there's to be consistency in character, there must be a common thread binding everything together. For us, this thread is obedience to Jesus' commands, instructions, and guidance as we seek and follow His will.

Christians are those people, and only those people, *who obey God*. In spite of errors and mistakes along the way, their lives can be characterized as consistently maturing into what God wants them to be. When all is said and done, they put aside personal desires, wants, concerns, dreams, and egos, sacrificing all to follow Christ. Through their love for Him, they adopt His desires, His wants, and His concerns. They grasp His vision and claim it as their own.

However, this isn't a role we simply step into and then discard when we're done. While we move through different changes in life, there is a definite and noticeable constancy. Christ is our foundation, and this foundation does not change. It brings to us a light through which others can see our witness to the world of the risen Lord.

Our witness to the world—sometimes we lose sight of what this phrase means. So often we think of faraway places, such as Africa or the Philippines, where for years many have labored. But Jesus never defined it that way. "'You will be my witnesses in Jerusalem, and in all Judea and Samaria, and to the ends of the earth'" (Acts 1:8b).

Jesus said His disciples would be His witnesses everywhere. Sure He wanted them to go to foreign and exotic lands—the ends of the earth. And He wanted them to go throughout their country and region—Judea and Samaria. But notice that the first place He mentioned was their own backyard, their hometown—Jerusalem.

Witnessing close to home was very important to Jesus. He also understood the difficulty in witnessing to those who know you. Remember the problems He had in Nazareth? Those people had known Him since He was a child. Because they wouldn't believe He could be so important, His ministry there was difficult.

Using the world's wisdom, this would be reason enough to discourage witnessing to those closest to us. The argument could easily be made that people should only be sent to places where they are unknown. It would be easier and more logical. We wouldn't have to be concerned that someone might see us only as a child or remember how we acted in the past.

But that's not what Jesus said to do. As He spoke to His disciples, He wasn't just telling them that His witness would spread throughout the world. He was also giving them a plan to follow. First, witness at home. Concentrate there before venturing beyond.

But why should this be the first place for our efforts? The answer is simple.

If we won't share the love, joy, peace, grace, and salvation of Christ Jesus with those we know and love, it will be impossible for us to bear the full witness of Christ to the world. Can we honestly reach out with compassion and hope to someone we've never met while turning away, with no thought or concern, from a mother or a brother, a next-door neighbor or a lifelong friend? Are we willing to risk our reputation or acceptance by those who know us well in order to show Jesus that we really do love Him?

Regardless of whether it's a neighborhood, country town, or bustling city, our first calling to witness is in our immediate community—where we live, work, and play. This is where we find out how much we care, and this is where the world watches closely to see if our witness and our God are for real.

Caring on Hold

Our witness to the world is defined, shaped, and affected as much by our inaction as by our actions. In fact, often what we fail to say speaks louder than words, and what we fail to do delivers a message greater than any action we could ever take.

Some time ago, the nation was shocked by the story of a murder in New York City. A woman, walking beside an apartment building, was assaulted and brutally stabbed. Her screams for help could be heard by many of the tenants, but they kept silent and did nothing. According to the police, she could have survived if someone had helped, but help never came, and she died on the streets.

A murder was committed that night, but who remembers the date or even the year? A woman's life was taken, but who recalls her name or anything else about her?

What we remember is the coldhearted callousness of some people in New York City, their total lack of caring and concern, and the disgust we felt towards them. More importantly, there are many who still recall that event whenever they think of New York City. Unfortunately, it has become their standard for determining how they feel about the people who live there today.

And the memory lives on. In 1995, a woman leaped from a bridge into the cold river below. According to the crowd that witnessed her death, she jumped out of panic when a man, who had assaulted her on the bridge, continued to pursue her. Though a few tried to help her after she jumped, no one in the crowd came to her aid on the bridge.

For several weeks, newspapers and magazines recounted each terrifying moment of the tragic tale. Detailed pictures showed the bridge, the woman's body being recovered from the river, a man being taken into custody . . . and all the faces in the crowd that would not help. In those many articles, we were asked to remember what had once occurred to a lonely woman in New York City.

People don't forget.

Using a single event to judge an entire group of people is unfair and wrong. Yet it occurs every day, often forming deep, long-lasting impressions. And it isn't limited to a murder in a large city. *It can also happen every time a casual Christian casts aside his religious robe and puts on the clothes of this world!* As his hypocrisy is exposed, those around may not recall his name, but they remember what he claimed to be. Then, just as in the

New York murder, they project their reaction to the event on the whole of Christianity.

We're also not talking just about total silence or inaction. We must remember the Christian context. Here we are referring to silence and inaction as they relate to Christian beliefs.

Consider the casual Christian's response to war. In 1991, the United States was in a military conflict with Iraq. We moved from the Gulf Crisis to the Gulf War and rallied around the banner of Desert Storm. Emotions ran high as we witnessed live bombing raids and heard generals plot targets and plan strategies. We saw some of our men and women killed and taken hostage. We rejoiced at the overwhelming victory and the return of our soldiers.

But there was one tragedy that occurred during this time that went virtually unnoticed: the failure by so many men and women to let others see Christ alive and at work in their lives *throughout* this ordeal. What did the non-Christian really see in the lives of those who claimed to follow Jesus?

They couldn't help but notice the churches overflowing at special services or the daily public calls for prayer, even from government officials who normally wouldn't allow such references in their buildings. Church support groups reached out to those who had spouses, children, and friends in the conflict. Signs, banners, and bumper stickers everywhere told us to "Pray for Our Troops."

Yet at the same time they saw these same people thrill with excitement at seeing our military bomb industrial centers, office buildings, and missile sites. They heard references to the deaths of Iraqi civilians as "just a part of war." They witnessed a *celebration* as tanks, troops, and transports passed through a desert littered with the bodies of enemy soldiers. What non-Christians really saw were casual Christians reveling in the glory of war—a glory that in reality did not exist and a war that was far, far away.

The point here is not to discuss the pros and cons of a military conflict, but to look at the witness presented by the casual Christian. During the Gulf War, he showed the world exactly what he thought of prayer: a tool to be used in a time of crisis to get something he wants, and a tool that, when the crisis is over, can be put back on the shelf. He also sent a strong message of what he thought of God: someone to turn to as a last resort but who can otherwise be ignored.

I'm afraid the world learned much from this display. The casual Christian prayed for peace and for God to bring about a swift and decisive victory, but when victory was declared and the soldiers came home, did this "Christian" keep praying? Did he really care? Is this how a God of love acts through His people?

To the unsaved world, the answers were clear—and through the silence and inaction that followed, the hypocrisy was painfully obvious.

TWENTY-SIX

The Reflection of Caring

The casual Christian strikes a direct blow to the true Christian witness. Often when he should be showing God's love and letting others see Christ in his life, there's only silence. He adopts the ways of the world, blending in so well that no one suspects that he occasionally claims to be Christian.

Then there are times when he jumps on that bandwagon. The cause is great and good. "We must help our unfortunate brother and sister," he cries. Unfortunately, the excitement can only be found in the *cause*. Concern, love, and caring, if present at all, are simply along for the ride.

The casual Christian develops his crusade for the *cause* in two ways. One involves only a small amount of effort on his part. This we will call the *Mouth Action Ministry*. The second, however, may require an enormous amount of time and effort. It is the *Misguided Crusade*.

The Mouth Action Ministry

The name gives away much of its meaning, but there was a time in my life when God let the full force of it hit home.

Some years ago as a young deacon, I was asked to preach at a mission church near my home. Now the thought of delivering a sermon had never crossed my mind, so I reacted with a normal, logical response: intense fear. I quickly chose the "Moses Method of Decision Making" and offered many reasons why I was the wrong man for the job. Unfortunately, I also had Moses' level of success.

Concerned that my entire relationship with God depended on this sermon, I spent many hours studying and planning. I prepared an outline, notes, cross-references, an outline of my cross-references, notes of my outline, and even cross-references of my cross-references. You might say I overdid it a bit.

On the morning of the blessed event, I sat in a Bible study class but heard very little of the lesson. All I could think about was *my* sermon and *my* delivery, what I was going to say and when I would say it, as well as all of the proper and recommended gestures and voice inflections. But then something happened.

God called my attention to a passage in Matthew. As I read the verses, He opened my eyes with *His* understanding. I'd read it many times before, but now there was new insight. God changed my entire sermon in about two minutes, and my outlook on caring for the rest of my life. This is His message: "When [Jesus] came down from the mountainside, large crowds followed him. A man with leprosy came and knelt before him and said, 'Lord, if you are willing, you can make me clean.' Jesus reached out his hand and touched the man. 'I am willing,' he said. 'Be clean!' Immediately he was cured of his leprosy" (Matt. 8:1–3).

I'd always read this as just another example of Jesus' power and authority, but I'd missed a very important point: true caring. Sadly, it's this point that the casual Christian continues to miss, causing great harm to the Christian witness in the community.

Jesus not only healed a man, He healed a leper. At that time, people who suffered from leprosy were seen as defiled and unclean. It was generally held that a leper was being punished by God for some sin in his life or within his family. He was, in every sense, a social and religious outcast. No one wanted to be near him.

To insure their isolation, lepers were forced to live in the unprotected areas outside the city. They even had to wear bells so others could hear them coming. The approaching clanging would warn "the clean and the righteous," giving them time to avoid any contact.

As the sick man came nearer, Jesus showed His followers the example of true caring. First of all, He stayed. He didn't run away or even turn to go. I'm sure the crowd had scattered and Jesus was alone. No self-respecting Jew would have allowed himself to be in the presence of a leper. Yet Jesus showed *compassion* by remaining and not ignoring this man.

Next, Jesus reached out and touched him. This must have shocked those watching. To touch an unclean person was forbidden by the man-made religious laws, which even made it a matter of personal and family shame. But Jesus clearly *communicated* that He cared for him. Love cannot be fully expressed by words alone. When the opportunity is there, we should be willing to touch others physically if we are to touch them spiritually. A hug often shows more concern than words ever can.

Then, Jesus told him He was willing to help. He expressed it verbally as a public statement for all to hear. This is important for us as well. It keeps us accountable for the task at hand, making it real and personal. When we hear ourselves say the words, it's no longer a passing thought. It has become a *commitment.*

Finally, Jesus healed the man. He followed through. He *completed* what He set out to do. He kept His word. Otherwise, everything else would have been meaningless.

God's message is simple: "I want you to follow My example. When a person needs help, don't run away. Take time to let him know I care for him and have sent you to show him My love. Reach out to him, become involved in his life, and let him know in every way that he is loved." *Caring, then, is compassion communicated through completed commitment.*

The casual Christian misses this entirely. He's too caught up in satisfying himself to be that concerned for someone else. His *ministry* is usually carried out with his mouth: lip service and nothing more.

An example of *Mouth Action Ministry* can be seen in his reaction to the homeless. There was a time, perhaps, when the average homeless person was just a man too lazy to work, refusing to meet his responsibilities. He was a wanderer, loafer, or hobo, and lived off what he could beg, borrow, or steal. Maybe it was his own fault that he came to such a state.

Once, perhaps, but no longer. More and more people find themselves homeless for reasons they could never have foreseen. They don't want to be homeless and desperately look for a way out.

I've come across a number of people who fit this description. There's Linda, a twenty-one-year-old woman who has three children. She married at seventeen and didn't finish high school. She never worked outside the home because her husband had a steady job and she took care of the children.

Then one day, her husband abandoned her and left the state. With no family to help, Linda tried to get a job, but no one wanted a high school dropout. Even being a waitress required experience using computerized cash registers. Besides, she couldn't afford the child care even if she got a job.

Linda was eventually evicted from her home. With her children in hand, she walked the streets, eating out of trash cans and sleeping in parks.

Then there's Ed, a man in his late forties and a former executive with a small advertising firm. The economy went bad and destroyed his business. The competition for work was so great that he couldn't find another position in the advertising field. Depression grew as he spent what little savings he had. No home, no car, no job, no future. He hit the streets only because there was nowhere else to go.

The plight of the homeless has been brought to the attention of Americans across the country. But what are we as Christians really doing?

The casual Christian often takes on the cause but fails to follow Christ's example. He talks a good game but doesn't follow through. Oh, he may nod in sympathy and sign a few petitions. He may even throw money at the problem, contributing to the efforts of another crusader, but he refuses to get personally involved. While he tells himself he's done his civic duty, he fails to meet a deeper, Christian responsibility.

He doesn't reach out to touch the man or woman to let them know he cares. He doesn't offer words of support, encouragement, or love. Instead, he crosses the street to avoid them and walks on by as they ask for food.

He applauds efforts to house and feed, but he's too busy to help. He gives awards to those who counsel, train, and educate these people for a better life, yet he himself doesn't have the time to give. He offers an occasional canned good or some old clothes, but he won't take them to a shelter or serve some meals.

It means something to really care for another person. It means *showing* that you care.

When I was ten years old, two weeks before Christmas, there was a short in the wiring of our house. Its spark started a fire that caused a lot of damage, and as a result, we were homeless. But we were very fortunate because there were people who cared for us and took us in. We lived with them for several months until our house was rebuilt.

There are some things in life you never forget, and I'll never forget that night. I can still see my dad struggling to put out a raging fire already out of control. I can still feel the cold as we stood barefoot in icy water with my mother crying, "I'm so sorry." And I can still see the tears in the firemen's eyes as they fought the flames.

But most of all, I remember a sincere love, caring, and concern that poured out for my family, especially for my brother and me. Among the tragedies for my parents that night was the destruction of all the Christmas presents they had bought for us. But because others cared, we got new presents from a speedy insurance agent, relatives, neighbors, friends at school, and my old Cub Scout pack, as well as from the College Park firemen. In fact, we got more that Christmas than I could ever begin to describe.

The toys and presents were great for two little boys, but they were not the greatest gifts. After all the years, I really don't remember the presents. But I do remember the love that was so desperately needed on a cold December night and that was freely given by so many people. That memory will be with me forever.

This is what God's love is all about. He wants us to share it and be involved in the lives of others. He's not satisfied when our participation is only reflected in a donation card. He's not pleased when our *love* consists of a ten- or twenty-dollar bill.

The Misguided Crusade

In his "helping my fellow man" role, sometimes the casual Christian gives more than lip service. A cause so celebrated or exciting comes along that prompts him to jump right in, exerting great effort to support it. This is the *Misguided Crusade*.

One that has captured the attention of millions is abortion. Few issues have caused such an upheaval in the Christian community. With just a mention of the word, caring individuals become hated enemies, a Bible study erupts into a shouting match, and congregations are divided. Dissension, factions, discord, and fits of rage develop among people who claim to be united in Christ.

To the casual Christian, this is perfectly acceptable. Why? Because of the *cause*. The cause is more important! It reigns. It rules. It supersedes. It justifies.

In 1989, a number of public forums were held around Atlanta concerning this issue. Whether abortion should be allowed or forever banned depended greatly on where the rallies were held. Certain communities, civic groups, and churches supported a woman having the option to choose abortion if she so desired. Other churches, parent organizations, and neighborhoods wanted a total ban, claiming such action constituted the taking of life and was, therefore, murder. Their meetings saw emotional speeches, angry outbursts, and calls to action.

Then came the protests. Many people blocked the entrances to abortion clinics. They lay down across roads, driveways, and sidewalks, refusing to allow passage. Others tried physically to restrain women from entering the facilities. Retaliation marches followed. These crowds were no different in their allegiance to their cause. During the marches, insults were hurled, taunting and ridicule of the other side spewed forth, and intense anger was expressed.

When the sides confronted each other, fights ensued and bricks were thrown. People were led away hurt and bleeding. Police officers wrestled marchers and protesters into vans and even kicked a few. People who claimed to be Christians were on both sides, arguing and fighting.

What's wrong with this picture? Were Christians acting any differently from the rest of the world? "The acts of the sinful nature are obvious: . . . hatred, discord, . . . fits of rage, selfish ambition, dissensions, factions. . . . I warn you, as I did before, that those who live like this will not inherit the kingdom of God" (Gal. 5:19–21).

Do Paul's words to the Galatians sound familiar? The casual Christian was in rare form back then, just as he often is when this issue is raised. As an onlooking world just shook its head, Satan had a field day.

How can we expect non-Christians to believe us when we tell them of Jesus' love and compassion—and then physically harm our own brother or sister? How do we explain that Christ lives in us and, through His Holy Spirit, we have access to His joy, peace, patience, kindness, goodness, gentleness, and *self-control*—when we abuse one another?

The casual Christian, of course, has no problem with any of this. After all, he checked his Christianity at the door when he left the sanctuary Sunday morning. He justifies his means by looking to a "worthy" end. He adopts the world's guide for action, confrontation, and conflict. And he clearly shows that prayer is only a last resort. For the casual Christian, the cause must survive above all.

Think what this attitude ignores concerning the issue of abortion: the emotional trauma of the pregnant teenager, the shame of her family, the emotion and guilt that often come after an abortion, the feelings of

the father, the conflict of rights between parents and children, the difficulty of raising a child by parents too young or resentful, and the emotional roller coaster ride we call adoption. Regardless of a person's
position on abortion, these are important issues. There must be love and
caring.

But for the casual Christian, such matters are for someone else.
When he keeps that child from having an abortion, he forgets about her
as she struggles with giving her child for adoption or trying to be a mature parent at sixteen. When he succeeds in protecting her "right" to an
abortion, he fails to help her when she suffers through doubt, or returns
to a lifestyle that ultimately brings her back to the clinic.

When we look at everything involved, does the casual Christian really care for the fetus he has saved or the girl who has aborted? Not really. He cares only for the cause, the fight, and his own satisfaction in
carrying out his personal desires.

Non-Christians look to our faith and our actions as evidence of the
truth of Jesus' teachings. When we don't follow them, we discount their
validity. "Otherwise," ponders a logical world, "they would pray and
have faith in their God." The true witness of Christ becomes blurred
when our faith is rooted in ourselves and our own abilities.

And so we shout and fight, instead of kneeling and praying. We di-
vide along battle lines, instead of joining together to seek God's will and
guidance. And above all, we promote the cause, often ignoring Jesus'
commands.

Showing the Love of Christ

One of the most powerful messages Jesus ever gave is the story of the good Samaritan. While Jesus was teaching, an expert in the law wanted to know how he could have eternal life. When Jesus asked for his opinion, this expert quoted the two greatest commands: "'Love the Lord your God with all your heart and with all your soul and with all your strength and with all your mind,' and, 'Love your neighbor as yourself'" (Luke 10:27). Although Jesus agreed, the man pushed further. He wanted to test Jesus, so he asked Him,

"And who is my neighbor?"

In reply Jesus said: "A man was going down from Jerusalem to Jericho, when he fell into the hands of robbers. They stripped him of his clothes, beat him and went away, leaving him half dead. A priest happened to be going down the same road, and when he saw the man, he passed by on the other side. So too, a Levite, when he came to the place and saw him, passed by on the other side. But a Samaritan, as he traveled, came where the man was; and when he saw him, he took pity on him. He went to him and bandaged his wounds, pouring on oil and wine. Then he put the man on his own donkey, took him to an inn and took care of him. The next day he took out two silver coins and gave them to the innkeeper. 'Look after him,' he said, 'and when I return, I will reimburse you for any extra expense you may have.'

"Which of these three do you think was a neighbor to the man who fell into the hands of robbers?"

The expert in the law replied, "The one who had mercy on him." Jesus told him, "Go and do likewise."

Luke 10:29–37

Sometimes we don't pay attention to what God is telling us in His Word, and we fail to understand. This is especially true of this story. We casually read the verses but only see God telling us to be nice to others.

But there's much more! Notice that the expert was stunned by this story. His words were brief and he didn't ask another question. Also notice that he couldn't even say the word *Samaritan*. What did this man hear that shocked him so much he could hardly respond?

The One in Need

First, take a close look at the man who was robbed. He was traveling alone from Jerusalem to Jericho, about a seventeen-mile trip. Hearing this, the expert would have immediately concluded the man was a fool. This road passed through rocky, deserted terrain known for thieves and murderers. If a man traveled that road by himself, he was asking for trouble.

How often do we see people like this? They go the wrong way or do the wrong thing. By their own foolishness or carelessness, they get into all kinds of trouble. This isn't just true for simple matters, like getting a car stuck in the mud or running out of gas. It also applies to very serious problems: divorce when a spouse has an affair; bankruptcy due to reckless financial ventures; a family destitute because the breadwinner dies with no insurance; jobs lost because of alcohol, gambling, or drugs; and so forth.

How do we often respond to situations such as these? "He's made his bed, now he has to lie in it." "It's her own fault. She wouldn't be in this shape if she'd listened to me." "I'm not lifting a finger. He's got no one to blame but himself."

What we're really saying is we're not going to get involved. We convince ourselves it will be too much trouble, the problems are justified, or it won't matter anyway. So we turn and pass by on the other side.

Yet when it came to caring, Jesus didn't count the traveler's foolishness against him. In spite of his actions, the Samaritan came to his aid.

The only thing that was important was that someone needed help. Also notice that the status or position of the hurt man didn't matter. By the time the Samaritan came along, he had been stripped of his clothes, robbed, and beaten so badly he was almost dead. The Samaritan couldn't tell if he was rich or poor, a priest or a thief.

Jesus never even says if this man was a Jew, a Roman, or another Samaritan. To the casual listener, the assumption was probably that he was a Jew, but I'm certain the expert caught Jesus' silence on this point. He heard the resounding lesson God was teaching: *It does not matter who or what the one in need may happen to be!*

The One to Help

As the beaten man lay there, three people came by. The first was a priest. By his position, he was a man of God, committed to following the Lord's commands. But when he saw the helpless victim, he passed by on the other side. Then came a Levite, a member of the tribe from whom the priests were chosen. Surely he was schooled in Scripture and intimately knew the letter of God's law. Yet he, too, passed by on the other side.

Only the Samaritan came to help.

For the expert, this was repulsive. Jews despised Samaritans as outcasts and half-breeds who didn't keep the Jewish law. In fact, Jews and Samaritans intensely hated each other. For two Jews to walk by and a Samaritan to be the hero was more than the expert could tolerate. But that didn't matter to Jesus.

God doesn't want our culture. He doesn't care about titles, social standings, jobs, education, or national origin. He wants us. He wants all of our heart, all of our soul, all of our strength, and all of our mind. Again Jesus' message hammered in the expert's ear: *It does not matter who or what you may happen to be!*

Involvement

Jesus wants action, not just words. Remember, He said, "'If you love me, you will obey what I command'" (John 14:15) and "'My command is this: Love each other as I have loved you. Greater love has no one than this, that one lay down his life for his friends'" (John 15:12–13).

The Samaritan took action. He came to the man, bandaged his wounds, and treated his injuries. He put him on his donkey and took him to an inn where he continued to care for him. This Samaritan didn't just talk about helping others, he actually did something about it. He sacrificed his time, his effort, and his resources to help someone he didn't know. He became involved in the life of another person.

Only one thing was certain. Here was a man who needed to be loved. The expert certainly understood: *We must be involved in the lives of those around us.*

The Neighbor

After telling the story, Jesus asked the expert a simple question: Who was the beaten man's neighbor? We may rush to answer, but the question itself requires close attention.

First, notice that Jesus didn't ask which of the three men was the good one, the nice one, or even the one more likely to get into heaven. Remember, the story was given to answer the expert's question, "Who is my neighbor?" If we're to love our neighbor as ourselves, then who is this neighbor? If we think only in terms of who is nice or good or even heaven-bound, we miss the point of the story. *Our neighbor is not defined in these terms!*

Also, Jesus didn't ask if the beaten man was the Samaritan's neighbor. Often teachers will make the mistake of referring to the beaten man as the neighbor. But this takes the focus off of the Samaritan. Jesus deliberately asked a different question: "Who was the neighbor to the beaten man?"

Now the expert in the law understood what Jesus was doing. He knew the importance of a question and how it was phrased. He knew, just as any good lawyer knows, that you often ask a question to make a point, not just to get an answer you already know. That's why he asked the questions to begin with. He already knew the answers. He just wanted to show Jesus how smart he was.

But Jesus knew better questions because He understood deeper answers. "Who was the neighbor to the beaten man?" By focusing on the Samaritan, Jesus sent another message to the expert: *You cannot be a neighbor by yourself. You can only be a neighbor in relation to another person!* To put it simply, if I'm your neighbor, then you must also be mine.

Many of us read about the Samaritan and look at his *goodness.* We remember the poor beaten man and think Jesus is telling us that others, like this man, are in need, that they are our neighbors, and that they need our care, so *we* name this story "The Good Samaritan."

This is true, but Jesus is also teaching us that we are their neighbors as well. A relationship exists whether we have ever met or not. A man standing alone can be a neighbor to no one. But where there are two, each is instantly the neighbor of the other.

What Jesus was saying, and what the expert clearly understood, was that a neighbor is someone even like the Samaritan: a man with a different religion, heritage, national origin—a man whose culture, politics, and moral beliefs are opposed to our own.

Who was the neighbor of the beaten man? The expert, unable to say the word *Samaritan*, could only refer to what he had done: "The one who had mercy on him." And it is here that we can easily miss Jesus' message.

Jesus did not agree with the expert! He never said a neighbor is the one who shows mercy. That was just the expert's answer, who, because of pride and prejudice, couldn't give credit to someone as lowly as a Samaritan, so he referred to him by describing his actions.

The Samaritan was the beaten man's neighbor, *but so were the priest and the Levite!* The difference is that through his love for the beaten man, the Samaritan *showed* love between neighbors. The priest and the Levite showed nothing at all. In every way, they failed to honor God's command.

Go and Do Likewise

Jesus' final instruction was a command: Go and do likewise. Whether or not the expert obeyed, we don't know. However, we do know that the command wasn't meant for him alone. Jesus issued this instruction to each and every Christian as a guide for how we're to live our lives, show our faith, and witness to the world.

Does this require us to look around for hurt and bleeding people on the side of the road? No, but this is essentially what we do when we join every charity drive that comes along. Many people interpret Jesus' command to mean we should be super-involved in social work, efforts to fight diseases, or a host of other causes. Unfortunately, they misunderstand what He's saying.

Jesus wasn't voicing support for social reform, charity organizations, or community projects. Nor was He downplaying such efforts. He was saying only one thing: *Love your neighbor as yourself, in whatever manner and in whatever opportunity that may be presented. Love each other and demonstrate this love with action. Love without action is not love at all.*

It is important to understand this command because so often well-meaning Christians, with the best of intentions, fail to fulfill it. In the story of the Samaritan, we have a better understanding of who our neighbor is, but we fall into the trap of defining love only in terms of what the Samaritan *did*.

Jesus was defining *neighbor*, not *love*. The Samaritan certainly showed the beaten man great compassion and love, but love is more than simply caring for physical needs. It is also the sharing of our faith.

TWENTY-EIGHT

Telling of the Love of Christ

Once during a meeting, a client made an interesting comment. He said, "Now, I'm not a Christian. I'm not saying anything bad about them, but I don't have time for that stuff and it's just not for me. But I do know that you are one and that you'll be honest with me."

Two things struck me about that statement. First, I was saddened by his casual disregard for not being a Christian. I couldn't help but think how horrible it must be to have a heart so hardened that it cannot hear the voice of God. Here was a man who spoke of Christianity as though it were a club or civic group. He didn't understand it as a fellowship of people called by God.

But secondly, though he could be so indifferent in his posture before God, even he had received some witness of Christ. He saw a Christian as one who would speak the truth. Now please don't misunderstand. This isn't a pat on *my* back. I had done nothing physically for this man. I never cared for him when he was sick or counseled him when he was lonely. I'd never had an opportunity to be involved in his life that way.

And yet, when our work brought us together, I had not hidden the fact that I am a Christian. Not that I gave a great sermon or made a special effort, but the fact that I'm a Christian and I believe certain things as a Christian was shown by the way I spoke and acted.

When we love our neighbor as ourselves, we are witnessing for Christ. When we show the kind of love He has shown, others will use that as proof that we are His followers, that we are real Christians. And this love must be more than action alone. When we do good deeds but never mention God, *we* get all the glory and God is ignored.

Give God the Glory

Though we may not want to admit it, this often occurs when we join a worthwhile cause, whether it's to raise money for leukemia research or provide shelter for the homeless. We struggle, work hard, spend countless hours, and, when it's all over, we take the bows! As we receive that plaque or special recognition, we're asked, "Why did you do it?" And then, when the greatest opportunity is presented, we smile, shuffle our feet, and tell the world, "Well, you know, these people were really hurting, and I'm just glad I could help."

Humble? No! We're telling the world that we took action because we're such nice people. But for a Christian, that's not the number-one, most basic reason why we do what we do. It's because God told us to. Pure and simple. The Christian is involved in the problems of the world because by doing so he's able to show people the love of God working through him in an effort to reach others for Christ.

We love our neighbor, just as we've been commanded by our Lord Jesus Christ. These are the fruits of His love in us. *And by this witness we prove that He exists!* When given the opportunity, we not only physically help others, but we also tell them of God's love and salvation in Christ. "'You are the light of the world. A city on a hill cannot be hidden. Neither do people light a lamp and put it under a bowl. Instead they put it on its stand, and it gives light to everyone in the house. In the same way, let your light shine before men, that they may see your good deeds and praise your Father in heaven'" (Matt. 5:14–16).

God works through us to reach a lost world and expects each of us to be a part of this witness so the world may see our good deeds and praise Him. If we don't tell them about God, it's impossible for them to praise Him. When they see us accepting the recognition and honor, not giving it all to the God we serve, they don't even know God was involved.

A Babel of Religions

Although there are many ways the Christian witness is affected in the community, there's one in particular which deserves special attention. Whenever I see it in a news report or magazine article, I can't help but recall the story of the Tower of Babel.

You remember the story. At one time there was only one language, so everyone could speak to each another. After wandering the earth, the early people of this world settled in the plain of Shinar and decided to build a tower. This tower was to be so great it would extend into the heavens. Though it would probably have been dedicated to God, its real purpose was to bring attention to the people themselves by showing off what they had done.

God saw in this human effort a people who believed they were capable of taking control of their destiny through the work of their own hands. Such reliance on self rather than on God could only lead to rebellion against Him. So God changed their language where they could no longer understand each other and scattered them throughout the world.

What reminds me of this story is the bonding today of different faiths, religions, and beliefs for the promotion of universal peace and harmony. Many applaud such efforts, pointing to the need for understanding and love. They claim that by tolerating the beliefs of others and focusing on the value of each person as a citizen of the world, all people can join together in a harmonious, loving relationship.

The casual Christian strongly supports such a "union." He rallies around its key ideals—peace, harmony, love, and understanding, but especially the idea of *self*-importance. This works so well with his desire for self-satisfaction that he becomes an avid disciple. However, I've reached a conclusion that may surprise you: Such a plan will never work. The effort to attain that goal at best has short-lived success and is usually a waste of time.

I've never understood why Christian men and women join such efforts. They involve very different people from many different lands who have very different beliefs. The problem lies in how we handle our own responsibilities. For example, since Christians are to witness to the world, do they use these efforts as an opportunity to share Christ? No, they don't. "That would be inappropriate. We must respect the beliefs of others and not cause any trouble."

I have a difficult time with this self-imposed restraint. First of all, Jesus told us to be His witnesses to the world. While every waking moment is not necessarily a time to evangelize, we should always *be* the example of Christ and be prepared to share Him with others. Do we really think Jesus would condone His followers belonging to an organization in which they agree *not* to witness for Him? I can't accept even the possibility that He would.

Also, as people work together in this new world order, friendships will develop. Only a casual Christian would keep silent about the salvation Jesus offers and let his friend to go to hell. A committed Christian would ache inside, knowing the horror that awaits his friend if he is not saved. *He could not keep silent!*

Within such movements are Catholic priests and Protestant clergy working side by side with Moslem, Hindu, and Buddhist leaders. They discuss the need for peace, fellowship, and harmony as well as world issues, such as poverty, famine, and disease. Everything appears on the surface to be a friendly joint effort for the common good.

But listen carefully to the statements being made. While Christian leaders don't immediately follow suit, their religious brothers tell the world that it's only natural for such cooperation to exist.

"After all," they claim, "there's only one God, one supreme being. The God of the Jew is the same God of the Christian. He is the same God of the Moslem and the same supreme being of the Hindu and the Buddhist. It's simply that each of us has his own way of describing and worshiping Him."

I find it amazing these same people don't realize that such philosophies are contrary to their own religions. For Christians, in particular, such ideas are heresy. There is only one God to be sure, but He is not what the Hindu makes Him out to be. The Moslem and the Buddhist don't come close to worshiping the God we know.

Such efforts for universal peace and love sidestep the very foundation of the Christian faith—the gospel of Jesus Christ. The function of every Christian is to obey Jesus, follow His example, and tell the world that He is the *only* way to eternal life. All other roads lead to destruction, yet, the gospel is ignored.

An incredible event in the fall of 1995 dramatically brought this into focus. Louis Farrakhan, an outspoken leader of the Nation of Islam, organized a massive gathering of black men in Washington, D.C., known as the "Million Man March." Its stated purpose was to unite African-American men in asserting personal responsibility, self-reliance, and commitment to family and community.

Many Christian leaders participated, loudly supporting Mr. Farrakhan's claim that the event was an ecumenical "day of atonement." While Christians were indeed present with their "Jesus" shirts and signs, what did non-Christians really see?

In the January, 1996 issue of *New Man* magazine, Gary Thomas and John Allen, two Christian journalists, told of their experiences at the march. Mr. Thomas wrote:

> Sheik Ahmed Tijuni Ben-Omar greeted marchers "in the name of Allah." The march was called a "holy day of atonement," and most of the orators had either "reverend" or "minister" attached to their names. Symbols of religion were prevalent all around.
>
> A Baptist pastor from Chicago read Psalm 51, followed by a Christian minister from Detroit who welcomed "Roman Catholics, Methodists, Baptists, Jehovah's Witnesses, and Muslims." Nation of Islam minister Rasul Mohammed chimed in, "It's no longer them Christians, them Muslims, but our Brothers."

Did anyone correct Ben-Omar's greeting or publicly challenge Mr. Mohammed's claim? Not according to the media. Mr. Allen struck at the very heart of the problem:

> I was encouraged to know that despite that day's pressure to put one's racial loyalty above all other beliefs, countless numbers of God's men would not conceal their Christian devotion. Sadly, though, of all the reverends and ministers to speak during the day, the only one to boldly mention Jesus was Farrakhan, who does not even acknowledge Christ as Lord.

The Million Man March had admirable goals in the eyes of the world, but it too felt the charges of racism fueled by an agenda whose direction was to separate people, not bring them together. In the midst were Christian leaders who joined with nonbelievers in calling attention to themselves (the Million Men) by showing off what they had done (the March). Instead of leading men to Christ, they pointed to themselves as the answer for their problems, saying, "Take control of your own destiny through the work of your own hands."

Sound familiar?

It's the Tower of Babel all over again. Men, bound by something in common, a desire for peace and harmony, seek their goals by relying on their own efforts. Because their beliefs are put aside, the world looks to their efforts and applauds them for what *they* are doing. The great effort is not for the glory of God. It's for the sake of mankind.

This doesn't mean that we should not cooperate in efforts for world peace, but we should understand that we are different. We don't have the same beliefs, nor do we worship the same. As followers of the risen

Lord, we cannot fall into the same trap as the casual Christian and try to change God into what we would like Him to be. We need to be true to Him and let others see that truth.

This Little Light of Mine

Jesus told us that we are the light of the world. If we hide that light, others will not see Him or know the joy and love of Christ in their lives. And we will have allowed another person to live without hope. Each of us is important in sharing this witness if we're to reach a lost world. After all, if they could find their own way, why would we call them *lost?*

Our light must shine for all to see, just like a beacon on a hill. Not so others may come to God through our individual efforts, but so God can work through us in reaching those who don't know Him. By seizing the opportunities God creates for us, we in turn can give opportunities for others to come to know and experience Him.

This is our mission as witnesses for Christ. We're not to take glory from God, but to give the glory to Him. He wants us to be involved in our community and in the world. He wants us to be a part of the efforts to help the poor and the sick, the homeless and the lonely. He wants us to share His love with others by being involved with our neighbors, regardless of who they may be.

As we care for others, raise money for causes, or educate the world concerning horrible diseases, we must also share a love that is God's alone, a love that was shown through the life, death, and resurrection of His Son so that everyone might have a chance to be reconciled with the Father and live in eternal peace with Him.

This is our witness to the world. This is the true witness of Christ. And by this witness, those who were once lost will say to the Christian: "For with you is the fountain of life; in your light we see light" (Ps. 36:9).

VIII

The Meantime

Yes, I am coming soon.

Revelation 22:20a

The Light of the World

Throughout this book, our focus has been the witness of God's people. We've examined the casual Christian and seen a self-centered life acted out according to personal desires. He may do good deeds and even join in Christian functions and organizations, but his heart ultimately seeks his own pleasure.

The casual Christian bears a false witness of what being a Christian is all about. The lost watch as he ignores his family and undermines the foundation of his marriage. They see him devoted to his work, pushing the welfare of others aside as he desperately climbs to the top of the heap. They applaud as he guides and leads causes designed to better the lives of people in this world—with no regard for the condition of their lives in the next. And they reward him with glory, honor, and praise for what *he* has done.

I've painted a pretty rough picture of the casual Christian, but God takes the matter of witnessing quite seriously. He doesn't condone the lies that the casual Christian carelessly gives the world. "A false witness will not go unpunished, and he who pours out lies will perish" (Prov. 19:9).

The casual Christian, in spite of the façade he has so skillfully built, is not a Christian at all. His words and deeds only give witness to his hidden belief that God, as described in the Bible, really doesn't exist. "To the pure, all things are pure, but to those who are corrupted and do not believe, nothing is pure. In fact, both their minds and consciences are corrupted. They claim to know God, but by their actions they deny him. They are detestable, disobedient and unfit for doing anything good" (Titus 1:15–16).

As we come to terms with God's reactions toward the casual Christian, we must also accept something else. Within each of us, there's a natural tendency to be a casual Christian. In some way, virtually everything that's been said about this person can also be said about each of us. We may find comfort in telling ourselves that we're not all that bad, but any degree of a false witness is intolerable in the eyes of God.

So then, should we give up and admit failure? No. But we should see ourselves for who we really are. Each of us has failures and weaknesses. No one is better than anyone else. We all fall far short of the glory of God.

Once we make this confession, we can focus again on God, develop a meaningful relationship with Him, and grow spiritually as He leads and guides our lives. We make mistakes, but unlike the casual Christian, we don't make them a regular part of our lives. They become the basis for more learning and more fellowship with our heavenly Father.

Our strength cannot be found in our arms or legs, but within the confines of our hearts, for there our desires to follow God are formed, and there His strength and His power can grow. We are simply to put forth real effort and do our best to seek Him and follow His will. "Do your best to present yourself to God as one approved, a workman who does not need to be ashamed and who correctly handles the word of truth" (2 Tim. 2:15).

We are the light of the world. If others are to see the truth, then that truth must be a part of our lives. God has warned us that the times will only get worse. Therefore, the need for a true witness, and our responsibility to provide it, are great.

I give you this charge: Preach the Word; be prepared in season and out of season; correct, rebuke and encourage—with great patience and careful instruction. For the time will come when men will not put up with sound doctrine. Instead, to suit their own desires, they will gather around them a great number of teachers to say what their itching ears want to hear. They will turn their ears away from the truth and turn aside to myths. But you, keep your head in all situations, endure hardship, do the work of an evangelist, discharge all of the duties of your ministry.

2 Tim. 4:1–5

It doesn't take a lot of effort to see the truth of these words in the world around us. Channeling, astrology, reincarnation, and the belief that we all possess godlike powers grow in acceptance every day, while Christianity is pushed further and further into the background. For many, worshiping the Christian God has become an embarrassment and the subject of scorn and ridicule.

Even in our churches we fail to look to Him. We have programs and projects that only show what we can do *for* Him, instead of what God can do *through* us. We claim His glory as we show the world how *we* have built *our* church.

But the day is coming when Jesus will return. There will be judgment and mercy, love and hate, eternal life and eternal hell. The hour is unknown . . . and there are still so many who need to experience the true witness of Christ. When He comes, it will be too late.

In the meantime, we must stand firm and bear witness to the world of who we are and what we believe. We must turn to God, submit only to His will, and become totally dependent on Him as He goes through time doing His work through us. In all things and in all ways, He must become greater in our lives as we become less.

When this happens, we will become God-centered and our witness powerful because God will be directing it. Through such a witness, others will come to know and experience a holy God . . . a God of promise and hope . . . a God of judgment and love . . . and a God of mercy and grace.

The writer of Acts begins, "In my former book, Theophilus, I wrote about all that Jesus began to do and to teach" (Acts 1:1). *All that Jesus began.* We should remember these words.

When He walked on this earth, Jesus *began* the great work of His ministry. He began to do wonderful things, calling God's children to Himself and sharing His teachings. If He began these things, it naturally follows that His work is continuing to this very day. And, in fact, it is!

Jesus' work continues in the lives of His disciples, His followers, and His friends. It isn't found in those who make token appearances on Sunday mornings, but in the men, women, and children who live Christlike lives *each* day of the week and in all circumstances, places, and times. Christ's work continues through those who dare to take a stand and let others know they are truly Christian.

May the grace of the Lord Jesus be with God's people as we . . . *take the stand.*